The Greatest Classroom Team Building Activities

A COMPLETE LESSON PLAN OF GAMES FOR EACH QUARTER

Paul Carlino

TABLE OF CONTENTS

DEDICATION

This book is dedicated to my wife and best friend Jamie. There is not a more beautiful, soulful person on this earth. You inspire me every day. This book would not have been written without your unwavering love and support.

I would like to thank the early pioneers of team building whose passion, innovation, and fun have encouraged me to see the value of experiential education.

I would also like to thank master teacher Lesa Meyer, whose creativity in team-building games has motivated me. And thanks to Dennis Lynch, who always pretended not to enjoy our team-building games, but was secretly the heart behind it all.

Lastly, to all my former students and athletes, thank you for enthusiastically enduring my new games and activities.

CHAPTER 1

WHY IS TEAM BUILDING IMPORTANT?

As a teacher, athletic coach, and class sponsor for thirty years, I have used the activities in this book in many different ways, for many different purposes.

Whether it is the beginning of a school year, the first couple days of practice, or a group meeting for the first time, it is important to find ways for individuals to get to know each other better. Icebreaker activities are simple and non-threatening ways to address this objective. Icebreakers that help groups mingle and mix in silly, fun ways can help make everyone comfortable. Once individuals in a group feel comfortable with each other, you will have a better chance of creating a learning environment. Push the boundaries. Challenge stereotypes. Deal with issues such as bullying, confidence, strategies to deal with problems, and teamwork. Often there are shy people in your class or team who do not mingle well or have the ability to let other people know who they are, or who have a hard time reaching out to get to know other people. Icebreaker activities will help mix all type of personalities, strengths, and groups.

TRUST/COMMUNICATION

As I coached basketball teams for eighteen years, I found that you could have the greatest athletes in the world on your team, but if they did not trust or communicate with each other they were not going to have a lot of success. Trust is not something that comes naturally to all people. Trust takes time. Trust takes communication. Through team-building activities that include trust and communication, you can not only be a better team player on the basketball court, but also you can be a better person off the court. The team-building lessons you do with your team, class, or group can transferred to working with people outside of the class, dealing with their home and life situations, or interacting with people in the future. Communication is one of those things that takes proactivity, and can be very challenging for many people. If you can teach a group or class to work together, to communicate, and to trust in a simple forum like a classroom or basketball field, think how much further they can apply the lessons they learned in work, home, relationships. Everything is transferable to life. You just have to help them make the connection.

SELF-ESTEEM AND PERSONAL BOUNDARIES

Self-esteem can be the one thing that separates a "successful" person from one that is "not successful." Self-esteem or lack of self-esteem can be rooted deeply in a person's family dynamics, as a result of abuse or failures. Wherever self-esteem is rooted, team-building activities can bring out strength in that person that they never thought they had. I have done team-building activities with students who had failed multiple classes, were not "popular," or were the target of bullying. I have seen students who have struggled with low self-esteem rise to the occasion, become leaders, and have success in the team-building activity. I have also seen other people in the group look at these kids and say, "Wow, I did not think he or she was such a leader." It really is amazing when you see a student who never speaks in class or can't make a basket become the leader of an activity, and take that activity over with their ideas, solutions, and leadership. These moments are what we live for as facilitators in team-building activities. To see someone push past their own personal boundaries—whether they be physical, emotional, or social—is the greatest feeling in the world.

LEADERSHIP

What is a leader? Ask ten different people and you will get ten different definitions. Leadership itself is a hard thing to define. To see it in action, to see someone lead, and to see a leader develop are some of the basic core beliefs and reasons why we do team-building activities. The old saying "leaders are born, not made" is not a philosophy that I believe in. Do I think that some people are natural leaders? Yes. Do I think that there are environments that enable or encourage some people to lead? Yes. Do I think that leadership can be taught, or modeled? *Yes.*

In doing team-building activities, it is amazing who steps up and leads. It's not always the loudest or most vocal member of the group. I have seen groups struggle to get through an activity, failing over and over again, until the one kid you would never expect to figure it out comes up with the solution.

Given the opportunity, most people can lead. Given an opportunity to see leadership, and be encouraged and supported, many can learn leadership traits.

Team-building activities are a nursery for leadership. Leadership traits that students learn now can benefit them years later.

SOCIAL, ECONOMIC, AND EDUCATIONAL ISSUES

As a teacher for thirty years in classrooms that have been mixed (socially, economically, and educationally), I cannot stress just how powerful and useful team-building can be in bringing together so many different groups.

Hot-button topics like bullying, religion, cultural differences, economic differences, and learning styles can all be addressed in team-building activities. Weaving together and addressing some of these very sensitive issues and topics through team-building activities, you can help your class, group, and team become a more cohesive group that respects and understands the differences they may have. On the flip side of this, through the course of these activities, group members may see that they have more in common with a group or culture than they ever imagined.

CHAPTER 2

HOW TO USE THIS BOOK

In writing this book, I wanted to create a team-building guide for the classroom. I have tried to keep it simple and easy to read and understand.

Having read many team-building books myself, I often found it difficult to understand conceptually how the activities looked or were run. In this book, there are numerous photos and diagrams that can help the reader understand how to run the activities.

Activities are divided into the four quarters of the school year. At the beginning of the year, the activities are relatively simple (e.g., name games, "getting to know you" games) and get more complex as the year progresses—building to high-end trust activities at the end of the year.

There are three major types of activities: icebreakers, cooperation and communication, and trust. Many activities involve two or more of these categories.

An overview of the various types of activities covered in this book follows. Use this as you begin to include team building in your classroom structure.

Before the activity categories are explained, a quick note about props will be useful. Props are anything you need to use such as a Hula-Hoop, balls, ropes, and so forth. Not all activities require props, but if you need props make sure you have them available. I would also recommend that you have extras available in case a prop breaks. There is nothing worse than having this great activity that requires a prop, but you don't have it, or it's broken.

ICEBREAKERS

Icebreakers are quick, fun, and low-maintenance activities that get a group energized. They could be as simple as a name game. There is not much processing or trust involved in these activities. Icebreakers are supposed to be fun activities that could be introduced at the start of the day. They can last anywhere from ten to twenty minutes.

COOPERATION AND COMMUNICATION

Cooperation and communication activities are experiences during which it is crucial for the group to work together and communicate in order to achieve success. Effective communication skills and the ability to cooperate are necessary attributes for success in today's world. These activities transfer easily from the classroom to the real world.

TRUST ACTIVITIES

These activities can be some of the most challenging for your group. Trust is hard to get, and even harder to accomplish in a group setting in which your students may not even know the people with whom they are working. While these types of activities are some of the most difficult to work through, they often yield the greatest reward and opportunity for meaningful processing.

Please note that safety is *always* the top priority when doing activities that involve trust. If the group does not feel safe, the members will have a hard time taking risks. It is your job as a facilitator to set the ground rules and clearly and firmly communicate these boundaries to your students *before* the activity begins. For example , you may set ground rules that no one can be lifted above the shoulders, or that if you are spotting you must use two hands at all times. It is a good idea to model or demonstrate to your students how to be a trustworthy spotter. With trust activities it is imperative that the group remains focused on the person or persons being spotted. When the group feels safe they will push their own boundaries, which can often lead to meaningful, significant processing later. There is nothing worse than doing a trust activity and having someone get hurt because of poor spotting or lack of attention. If there is no trust, there is no risk, and if there is no risk there cannot be any growth.

WHAT IS PROCESSING?

Processing questions are what the facilitator asks during and after the activity. Not all activities need to have intense processing. Some activities, such as quick energizers, do not really need much processing. Other activities will need a lot of processing. In processing, your focus should be on listening to your students rather than talking to them. Try to get a feel for their perception of the activity. Increase your understanding of them as they increase their understanding of each other.

Examples of processing questions are:

- How did you feel while the activity was going on?

- What did you struggle with?

- What did you learn about yourself?

- What did you learn about the group?

- What would you do different?

- Did you feel supported by the group? Why or why not?

- Did you feel safe?

- Did you feel your input was listened to and respected?

- How could you apply what you learned in this activity?

- Have you ever felt like giving up? How did you get over it (or not)?

It is important to remember that during processing you have to feel the group, read the group, and anticipate opportunities to process what they are doing and relate it to "real life" experiences.

If they cannot relate it to real-life experiences, then what you are doing is just a game. Working through processing questions is hard to do and takes practice. If you focus on processing questions for too long, you will lose the group.

When processing, be cautious not to talk too much. Ask questions that will open up dialogue between the group and individual. Guide them, but let them find their own meaning.

The following are suggestions of how to use activities during the course of a school year.

- ➤ The first quarter of the school year you want to start out with easy, low-risk icebreakers such as name games.

- ➤ Quarter two will include simple icebreakers with the introduction of activities that require more teamwork.

- ➤ Quarter three continues with icebreakers and moves to more communication and cooperation activities.

- ➤ The fourth quarter will move to some harder and deeper activities that will have some powerful processing topics. Trust activities will be a big part of the fourth quarter activities. By the fourth quarter of a school year you will know your class well, and the trust activities provided will be a great way to close out the school year.

CHAPTER 3

IS LEADING A GROUP AS HARD AS IT LOOKS?

Leading a group takes time. If you have never led a group before, you have to give yourself permission to make mistakes. The key is to not overthink it. Be true to yourself, and have fun. Too many times the leader/facilitator of a group tries to provide all the answers. It is very easy as a facilitator to want to jump in and give "hints" when the group is struggling.

While this may make you feel better, it is actually interfering with the group's ability to process information, work together, and come up with a strategy to solve the problem at hand. As a leader, your job is to take the group out of their comfort zone and encourage them to use teamwork, communicate, problem solve, and develop trust within the group.

STARTING OFF

How you present yourself and the challenge during the first ten to twenty minutes of any activity will set the tone for how the group perceives the task and your leadership.

> ➢ Put yourself out there and let them know you are not above any of them or what you are going to ask them to do.

> ➢ Make sure your directions are clear and simple.

> ➢ Tell them a little bit about yourself, your background.

> ➢ Get involved in the activities and don't act like you are better than the group members.

> ➢ Laugh and smile, and enjoy. If you're not having fun, they won't have fun.

WHAT THINGS CAN AFFECT HOW I DEAL WITH A GROUP?

In twenty-nine years of running groups I cannot remember one template that worked well with all groups. There are several factors to consider when working with and evaluating how you plan to run your group.

AGE

The age of the group members can dictate what activities you choose to do, how long the activity should last, and how much processing you do afterward. With younger kids, be aware that they will have a shorter attention span. For students age ten and under, keep the activities less than thirty minutes. The energy level with younger kids needs to be at a high level all the time. As with any age group, you must be willing to adapt quickly.

CULTURAL

You must be able to understand various cultural differences. Characteristics of certain cultures may not be accepted by others. For example, being of Italian descent, I grew up in a family where hugging was a part of our daily ritual. The noise level in my house on any given day would exceed the acceptable standards at a rock concert. Part of team building is asking participants to sometimes go outside their comfort level to achieve a team goal. It is important in supporting this objective to be sensitive to how different cultures interact and function.

GOALS

Each group has different goals. Some programs are looking for a "fun" day away from the "normal"—where students can intermingle, laugh, and have fun while also strengthening the "team bond." Other programs are looking for a more intense day where team members need to succeed together and on their own to achieve a common goal.

As a facilitator, sometimes you want a group to succeed so badly that you have them do it your way or offer suggestions to help them be successful. While wanting a group to succeed is normal, sometimes it is in the best interest of the group to sit back and not say much and let them figure it out. A facilitator's input is valuable, but it can take away how the group perceives their successes as well as their failures. There are situations where I have given hints or input on how to work through things, and then they have failed, and the failure was my fault. When I got my counseling degree, the best advice I ever got from my clinical was when one professor told me, "Paul, counselors don't give advice. They listen, and help guide the people they are working with to solutions they already know, or have the ability to solve on their own." The same is true of facilitating team-building activities.

CHAPTER 4

HOW DO YOU LEAD A GROUP?

Now that you are almost ready to lead your group, I'm sure there are some questions you many have, such as:

➢ How do I start the session?

➢ What games do I choose?

➢ What are the key components of a successful group?

➢ How does one set goals and know what direction to lead the group?

Let me start with the most basic of all concepts.

FUN: What you are doing should be fun and have a purpose. If you are not having fun, your group will not have fun. They have to see that you are as into the activity as you expect them to be. They will be looking to you to set the tempo. If you come out flat, it could set the tempo for a flat day. The first activity that you choose should be a simple one, one that does not require a lot of trust or a lot of teamwork. You don't want your group getting burned out on the first activity. We call these first activities "icebreakers.".

These activities should last anywhere from five to twenty minutes. Again, they should be low on trust and high on energy and laughter, low on teamwork and high on fun. A good activity to start your day would be some sort of name game. I have included many versions of name games later in this book. Your ability to communicate in the beginning what you expect from them, how the day will go, and how the activity will proceed is crucial. A warm, fun facilitator always is much more effective than a serious or strict facilitator.

Always remember (especially early on) to invite them to participate. *Do not demand* that they participate. There may be some individuals that are apprehensive about group activity, physical activities, or close body contact. I start every day by asking if there are any physical limitations. Some people may have injuries that are not obvious such as a bad back, recent surgery, and so forth. You need to be aware of those, not only for liability reasons but also for personal safety. You may also ask if anyone has had any experience with team-building/group activities and how they felt about it and why.

If you see one or two people "bossing" or demeaning other group members because they are not doing well, or not doing it the way they think it should be done, you need to stop the group and deal with it *immediately*. This can be handled in many ways. You do not want to come across as punishing to any students. You want to deal with it by saying things such as, "What I am seeing is…"or asking the person being attacked or demeaned, "How are his directions making you feel right now?" These situations can be easy to defuse if handled the right way.

If you allow this member to dominate the group, other group members will not participate any longer. They will simply defer to the ones giving the directions. That is why you must constantly monitor and guide the group, not only in the activity but in who is communicating.

I often see a very quiet person trying to give their ideas, but they cannot be heard over the group. It is OK to let this go on for a time; you need to judge for how long. At some point you may stop the group and say, "Here is what I am seeing. There are some really good ideas that I have heard, but as a group you don't appear to be listening." I may then ask the individuals that have not been heard about their ideas, and how it made them feel that no one was listening to them. Then I would address how it feels as a whole to not be heard.

If people are having fun and enjoying themselves, then they are motivated, engaged, and open to higher learning concepts.

There are natural ebbs and flows of the group activities. It is normal for the group, especially when struggling to get through an activity, to begin to give up or have a drop in their energy level. Do not take this personally, but be wary of when it is happening, and modify the activity by taking time to process what you are seeing. Address their issues or frustrations, help them to get back on track, and try to bring the fun back into the group. Personal stories of successes, failures, or goofy stories can take the emphasis off of the struggles they are having and lighten the mood.

There is no one way, right way to run a group. Every group is different from the next. The one thing that is consistent is you— your energy level, your love for what you are doing, your desire to help the group achieve, redirect, laugh, and have fun. It is a huge responsibility to facilitate, and an even larger task to always keep the energy level up. At the end of a day of facilitating I am *exhausted*. I literally walk away having given every ounce of energy. If you walk away with lots of energy, you have not given your best effort. You *must* be willing to adapt, listen, and laugh with the group. You must also sincerely feel their frustration on some activities and be able to guide them while not talking over the group.

In short, you have to juggle many balls at one time to be a great facilitator. There just is no taking off from an activity because you are tired. They are looking to you for guidance, energy, and fun. *You must* deliver.

CHAPTER 4–1ST QUARTER GAMES

BALL TOSS

GAME TYPE
Icebreaker

MATERIALS
Any type of ball—tennis, golf, baseball.

GROUP SIZE
10–15

TIME
10–20 minutes

OBJECTIVES
This simple game can be played as an icebreaker at the beginning of the school year. The object of this game is for people to move around, learn some names, and get to know each other. It can be played inside (you will need higher ceilings) or outdoors.

INSTRUCTIONS
1.   Organize the group in a circle.
2.   The facilitator should begin the game by calling out their own name while tossing a ball to the person on their right.
3.   The person with the ball then calls out his or her name and tosses the ball to the person to their right. This continues until the ball has

made it all the way around back to the facilitator.

4. Now the fun begins! The facilitator throws the ball to *anyone* in the circle calling out their name.

5. The student that catches the ball repeats this until everyone has a turn or two.

PROCESSING QUESTIONS

How did it feel to have the pressure to remember the names of people you may not know? Have you ever been in situations where you did not remember someone's name? If so, how did you handle it? Did you use tricks to remember their names?

NAME LINE-UP

GAME TYPE

Icebreaker; cooperation and communication

MATERIALS

A piece of masking tape that can be used as a line

GROUP SIZE

6–15 per group (multiple groups play at one time)

TIME

10–20 minutes

OBJECTIVES

This is a simple name game that can be played anywhere. The objective is for students to communicate and work together to line up in alphabetical order (first or last) without speaking or stepping off the line.

The greatest part of this game is not allowing anyone to talk, and encouraging creativity. You can have multiple groups do this at the same time. Make it a fun competition.

INSTRUCTIONS

1. Put down a piece of masking tape, or use the straight line of a tile to act as a guide. If you are outdoors, you can use a log or bench to make this game more challenging.

2. Communication must occur through hand gestures or other nonverbal methods, like mouthing the words. Participants are not allowed to completely step off the line; one foot must be on the line at all times.
3. If anyone speaks or steps off the line, the game starts over.
4. Time the groups to see how fast they can accomplish the task.

VARIATIONS

There are many types of variations possible, including:

- Birthday
- Middle name
- Birth city or state
- Height
- Shoe size
- Birth date
- Middle names
- Number of bones broken
- Number of siblings

PROCESSING QUESTIONS

How did it feel when you needed to start over? Did your group work together? Was it hard to communicate nonverbally?

M&M GAME

GAME TYPE
Icebreaker; processing

MATERIALS
M&Ms (make sure no one has any food allergies before you start this game)

GROUP SIZE
10–20

TIME
10–30 minutes

OBJECTIVES
The objective of this game is to get participants to share personal information—based on the color of an M&M.

I have learned a lot about my students from this simple fun game. The questions for the each color are totally up to you and what you are looking for.

INSTRUCTIONS
1. Before playing, develop a game where each color of M&M represents a different topic. For example, for every blue M&M you have to tell us something about yourself, for every yellow M&M you have to tell us something about your family, for every brown M&M you have to tell us about something for which you are proud, for every green M&M you need to tell us something you are worried about.

2. Open a bag of M&Ms and give the students a handful—making sure everyone gets a variety of colors. You could also divide the candy into groups, ensuring each student gets one M&M of every color.
3. Once the M&Ms are handed out, write the key to the colors on the board, or pass out a piece of paper communicating what each color of M&M represents.
4. Each student then goes through their pile of M&Ms and shares information about themselves based on the key.

You can customize the questions based on the type of group. If you want it to be sillier and fun, make the questions more lighthearted. If you are looking for more in-depth information, make the meaning of each color more meaningful and deeper.

VARIATIONS
Other candies, colored cereal, poker chips, etc. can be used rather than M&Ms.

PROCESSING QUESTIONS
Did you find it hard to share personal information? If yes, why? What was the most interesting thing you learned about your classmates that you did not know before? Did you find it hard to share personal information?

RUBBER-BAND ROUNDUP

GAME TYPE
Icebreaker; processing

MATERIALS
A bag of rubber bands (not the thick type).
They must be long enough to fit over your head.

GROUP SIZE
10–30

TIME
10–15 minutes

OBJECTIVES
Students will get the rubber band from their upper to lower lip without touching it.

INSTRUCTIONS
1. Organize everyone in a circle (seated or standing).
2. Hand out a single rubber band to each person.
3. Demonstrate to participants how to place the rubber band over their head, and over their upper lip. The rubber band may need to be over the ears, as it may be easier to achieve the outcome.
4. Ask everyone to face a person next to them.
5. Now instruct the group that the object is to get the rubber band from their upper lip to their lower lip *without* using their hands. *Now* the fun begins!

The fun is not only in trying to achieve this goal, but also in looking at the people around you and their faces while trying to achieve the same goal.

PROCESSING QUESTIONS

Did you have fun doing this activity? Do you have a hard time being silly? What is the silliest thing you have ever done in your life?

SMILE WARS

GAME TYPE
Icebreaker

MATERIALS
None

GROUP SIZE
10–30

TIME
2–3 minutes/round

OBJECTIVES
Make a classmate laugh. This game is designed to have the students interact with each other in a very simple manner, and to have fun.

INSTRUCTIONS
1. Have your students turn their desks so that they are facing each other in pairs.
2. Instruct the class to try to make the person they are facing smile or laugh first by making funny faces, or doing any type of gestures (that are appropriate).
3. The student that doesn't smile or laugh "wins" the round.
4. Once a student wins you can have them stand up and move to another desk with another winner and have them compete. You can keep doing this until you have a "champion."

It is amazing how much fun the students have doing this.

VARIATIONS
You can challenge other classes and their champions. You can award prizes to the "ultimate" champion.

I like to use this in the last ten minutes of a Friday class before the week is over. Make it special and the students will look forward to SMILE WARS.

PROCESSING QUESTIONS
Do you have a hard time doing silly activities around other people? What are some of the silliest things you have done in front of someone? What do you do to get others to laugh? What makes you laugh?

I KNOW I AM, BUT WHAT ARE YOU?

GAME TYPE
Icebreaker

MATERIALS
None

GROUP SIZE
10–20

TIME
10–15 minutes

OBJECTIVES
Students will get to know names in a fun way.

INSTRUCTIONS
1. Have your class get into a circle.
2. Start out by saying an adjective with your name (make it fun and appropriate). For example, playful Paul.
3. The person to your right then has to say your name with the adjective you used, and then add an adjective to their name. For example, terrible Tommy.
4. The name game continues with the person to the right, who says the name of the first person with the adjective, and going around until they say their own name with an adjective. This continues until you go around the circle. This name game ends when it

gets back to the person who first started the game. The last person in the circle has the hardest job, as they must remember every adjective and name.

VARIATIONS
You can have the group build a story with the names as they go along. For example, playful Paul and terrible Tommy were at the store when they ran into jumpy Judy... continuing on until all the names have been used up in the story.

PROCESSING QUESTIONS
How do you remember people's names? What do you do when you meet people again and forget their name?

COAT OF ARMS

GAME TYPE
Processing; icebreaker

MATERIALS
Construction paper, markers, pictures from magazines, personal photos

GROUP SIZE
Any

TIME
30–40 minutes

OBJECTIVES
Students will express themselves and teach others about their lives.

INSTRUCTIONS
Have each individual student make a coat of arms (see diagram on next page). The students can design the coat of arms and add pictures, artwork, and photos.

Display the coats of arms on the walls of a classroom or in the hallways for all classes to see. This is a great activity for the first month of school.

In the six sections of the coat of arms you can have your students put the following descriptions in the sections.

1. A symbol or picture to represent an important place in your life
2. A symbol or picture of a hobby or activity that you enjoy
3. An animal that represents you
4. A personal motto (words or phrases that represent you)
5. A picture or drawing of the people in your family

You can use these lists as a guide and add anything that you feel would help your students describe themselves.

PROCESSING QUESTIONS

What did you learn about yourself and your classmates in designing your coat of arms? If you design this again twenty years from now, how might it look?

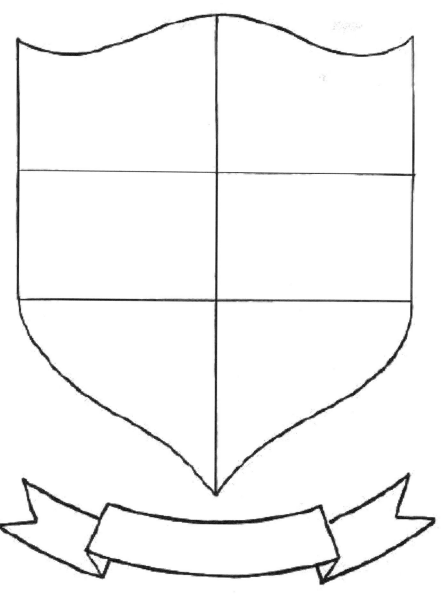

COAT OF ARMS DIAGRAM

PASS THE HOOP

GAME TYPE
Cooperation and communication; icebreaker

MATERIALS
Hula-Hoop or a piece of string (4–5 feet long) tied in a circle

GROUP SIZE
10–50

TIME
10–20 minutes

OBJECTIVES
The object of this game is to get the Hula-Hoop or string around, over, and through each person until it has gone around the circle. Working as a team and communication are essential to being successful in this game.

INSTRUCTIONS
1. Gather the group in a circle (standing).
2. Ask everyone to hold hands with the person next to them.
3. Pick a starting point and get either a Hula-Hoop or a large string tied together so it is in the shape of a circle.
4. Unlock the hands of two students, place the Hula-Hoop/string between their hands and have them return to holding hands.

5. Without unlocking hands, the Hula-Hoop/string has to be passed over the body, over the arms, and to the person to the right, all without breaking the hands apart.
6. The Hula-Hoop/string has to make it all the way around the circle.

VARIATIONS

*   Add in more Hula-Hoops/strings (1–3) and instruct the students to pass them in different directions at the same time.
*   Have competitions to see which section can pass their Hula-Hoop/string around the circle faster.

PROCESSING QUESTIONS

What was the hardest part of this activity? Did your group communicate well in order to achieve the goal? How did you feel when someone in your group had a hard time doing the activity? How do you deal with people in your life who are not working as hard as you are?

BIRTH ORDERS

GAME TYPE
Icebreaker, communication

MATERIALS
Paper, pencils

GROUP SIZE
10–30

TIME
10–30 minutes

OBJECTIVES
The object of this activity is to for students to talk about their families, birth orders and characteristics, and how they are alike or different from others.

INSTRUCTIONS
1. Start out by talking about birth order and how people of the same birth order sometimes share similar qualities.
2. Create four birth-order groups. Ask students to gather with their appropriate group (oldest, youngest, middle, only child).
3. Create a fifth group for students who don't fit into one of these groups.
4. Ask each student to write up a list of characteristics that *they* think best describe their own group.

5. Once their lists are complete, ask a member from each group to read their list to the rest of the class. You may want to write some of these characteristics on the board for discussion later.

6. When the lists are complete, go over which characteristics they have in common.

VARIATIONS

List common birth-order traits on the board and ask the students to guess the category.

PROCESSING QUESTIONS

How are you impacted by birth order? Did you find you had the same qualities as others in your group? Did you find yourself having any qualities that other birth orders did? Which birth order group do you get along with or work best with? Why? What did you learn about the other groups? What birth order do you wish you were born into?

I'M GOING ON A TRIP

GAME TYPE
Processing; icebreaker

MATERIALS
None

GROUP SIZE
10–20

TIME
10–20 minutes

OBJECTIVES
This activity is a great one for finding out things that are special or important to your students.

INSTRUCTIONS
1. Start by telling the group that they are going on a trip and they can only pack one bag. Tell them the size of the bag (i.e., backpack, duffel bag). Let them know that the bag can contain *anything*.
2. Ask them to make a list of the things that they are going to put in their bag, and explain why they chose those items.

VARIATIONS
- Ask the students if they could only bring one item, what would it be?
- If they could bring one person on the trip, who would it be and why?

PROCESSING

Have you ever gone somewhere and forgot to bring what you needed?

How do you organize your day? Do you make a check list or just wing it?

How can you be better organized?

What do you do when you find yourself in a situation and your not prepared?

TIC-TAC-ME

GAME TYPE
Icebreaker; cooperation and communication

MATERIALS
Tic-Tac-Me cards for each student (on next pa)

GROUP SIZE
10–30

TIME
5–15 minutes

OBJECTIVE
This activity will help students get to know their classmates.

INSTRUCTIONS
1. Customize the Tic-Tac-Me card and create enough for the entire class.
2. Hand out a Tic-Tac-Me card to each student.
3. Tell the students that they must walk around the room and find someone that matches a trait on the Tic-Tac-Me card. Once they identify a student with one of the traits, that student should sign their name on the spot where the trait is listed.
4. The first person to get 3 boxes in a row wins.
5. The same person cannot sign more than one space on the card.

VARIATIONS

The same game can be played with a bingo format (rather than tic-tac-me). You can create any tic-tac-toe card you want with many variations of questions.

PROCESSING QUESTIONS

What did you learn your classmates? What were you most surprised to learn?

TIC-TAC-ME SAMPLE CARD

I have more than 3 siblings.	I met a famous person once.	I can touch my nose with my tongue.
I can juggle.	I went out of my state on a vacation last year.	I have more than one pet at home.
I have broken a bone.	I have moved more than 2 times in my life.	I play an instrument.

PARTNER STAND-UP

GAME TYPE
Icebreaker; processing; cooperation and communication

MATERIALS
None

GROUP SIZE
Groups of 2

TIME
5–15 minutes

OBJECTIVES
This activity will help students learn teamwork, trust, and communication in order to reach a common goal

INSTRUCTIONS
1. Pick a partner.
2. Sit on the floor with your back against your partner's back.
3. Lock your arms and attempt to stand up by pushing back on the other person for support.
4. Once this is achieved, turn and face them, still sitting down, soles of the feet pressed together.
5. Hold hands and attempt to stand up together by pulling on your partner.

VARIATIONS

- Try doing this same activity with groups of four and six—sitting in a circle and linking arms.
- Try this same activity in reverse position. For example, start standing and try sitting down together.

PROCESSING QUESTIONS

How did it feel to trust someone? Do you struggle with trust and if so why? Did you feel your partner was working as hard as you to achieve this goal? If not, how did you work it out? Have you had to work with someone in another situation that you did not know? Did you feel they were working as hard as you? If not, what did you do to work through it? How do you deal with situations when you are frustrated?

WE ARE ALL CONNECTED

GAME TYPE
Icebreaker; processing

MATERIALS
None

GROUP SIZE
10–40

TIME
10–20 minutes

OBJECTIVES
Students will become more aware of other people around them and the traits they all have in common. This activity is great for beginning dialogue about cultural defenses, social differences, and "cliques."

INSTRUCTIONS
1. Talk to the group about how sometimes when we look at someone we think we are very different from them, yet as we get to know them better we realize that we actually have more in common with them than we ever realized.
2. Start this activity by making a statement about yourself. For example, "I have over fifteen pairs of shoes."
3. Ask everyone in the room who shares this trait to come up and hold hands or link arms.

4. Ask the person to your right to make a statement about their life. For example, "I have been to Disneyworld." Remaining students who have that trait should join the group—holding hands or linking arms.
5. The game continues until everyone is "linked up."

VARIATIONS

This game can be changed to be similar to Twister. Rather than only linking once, students can "link" to each person with whom they share a common trait. If they are already holding hands or linking arms, they must figure out how to touch the next person who shares their trait (though a foot, head, or body lean).

PROCESSING QUESTIONS

What were you most surprised to learn about (name a classmate)? Do you tend to write people off that you either don't know or think are different from you? Have you ever been written off by a person or group just because outwardly you did not fit in, or they did not give you a chance to get to know you? How does it feel to be rejected by a group you want to be a part of, or a person you want to know?

COUNT-OFF

GAME TYPE
Icebreaker

MATERIALS
None

GROUP SIZE
10–40

TIME
10–20 minutes

OBJECTIVES
Students will have fun and learn patience.

INSTRUCTIONS
1. Start this game by telling your class you are going to start counting.
2. You will start by saying the number "*One.*"
3. Someone in the class will randomly say, "*Two.*"
4. Another person in the class will randomly say, "*Three.*"
5. If any two students say the same number at the same time, the game needs to start over.
6. Each student should only say one number.
7. The students may not look at each other while counting off.

VARIATIONS

Keep track of the time it takes to get through the entire class count without starting over. Keep that record on the board.

PROCESSING QUESTIONS

Were you ever frustrated when you needed to start over? If so, how did you deal with it? How do you handle failing at things? What are some of the things you have failed early and then come back and been successful at? What failures are you still trying to overcome?

I'M A SCORPIO...WHAT ARE YOU?

GAME TYPE
Icebreaker; processing

MATERIALS
Horoscope from local paper

GROUP SIZE
10–30

TIME
15–30 minutes

OBJECTIVES
This activity will help students better understand the common traits they have with other people and how they may impact whom they choose as friends

INSTRUCTIONS
1. Talk about astrological signs. Read your own horoscope from the local paper for the day.
2. Have your class divide up into groups based on their astrological signs. It may be helpful to list the signs and associated dates on the board.
3. Once the students are in their groups, ask them to come up with a list of traits that they have in common.
4. Once all the groups complete their lists, ask one person to come up to the board or overhead and write the traits under their sign.

5.   Once all the groups have identified their traits, circle the ones that different groups have in common.

VARIATIONS

List a trait and have the class guess the associated sign.

PROCESSING QUESTIONS

Did most of the people in your astrological sign have a lot of common traits? Do you feel you get along better with people in your own sign, or do you see another group that you tend to get along with better? If so, what traits in other groups do you like? Do they parallel the people you hang out with or like to be with? Is there a group or trait that you have a hard time working with, or getting along with? And if so, why? What can you do to better get along with people with different traits?

IT'S CONTAGIOUS!

GAME TYPE
Icebreaker

MATERIALS
None

GROUP SIZE
Groups of 6–10

TIME
5–15 minutes

OBJECTIVES
Students will have fun and interact with other members of the class while learning everyone's names.

INSTRUCTIONS
1. Talk to your class about diseases that are contagious, such as the flu, measles, and chicken pox.
2. Divide your class in groups of 6–10, and have them get into circles.
3. Start the game by introducing yourself and adding an imaginary ailment. For example: "My name is Paul and I have a twitchy right eye."
4. The next person in the circle then introduces the first person. For example: "This is Paul and he has a twitchy right eye." After the introduction, that next person acts out the first person's ailment. Then they move on to

introduce themselves and their ailment. For example, "I'm Sara and I have a foot that taps."

5.	The game continues with each new person making introductions, starting with the first person and acting out their ailment, then introducing all the other people and acting out their ailments until the entire group has gone. The last person will have the toughest job because they will introduce everyone in the group and their associated ailment.

VARIATIONS

- You can have one member of each group introduce each student and their ailment to the other groups.
- During the school year, the teacher can randomly act out one of the ailments and see how long it takes the class to understand what is happening.

PROCESSING QUESTIONS

Which "ailment" was the most fun to act out? Have you ever seen anyone with an ailment, such as a tic? How did you react to it? Do you avoid or make fun of people with tics, or have you seen people make fun of people with tics? How does that make you feel?

DETECTIVE

GAME TYPE
Icebreaker; processing

MATERIALS
None

GROUP SIZE
Groups of 2

TIME
10–20 minutes

OBJECTIVE
Students will see how much detail they retain when communicating with another person.

INSTRUCTIONS
1. Have your class pair up in groups of 2.
2. Ask each person to face their teammate and stare at each other for 30 seconds.
3. After 30 seconds, have them turn back to back and describe the following: eye color, hair color, jewelry, hair length, shirt color/ description, etc.
4. After each person finishes the description, ask the students to switch partners and repeat the exercise.

VARIATIONS
Make this game a competition. After each round, create pairs based on the number of correct

answers. Continue until you can crown a champion.

PROCESSING QUESTIONS

Did you pay more attention after each round? Will you remember more details about your classmates after this activity? When you first meet someone, what do you look at? Where is your focus?

MY PERSONAL TIME CAPSULE

GAME TYPE
Icebreaker; processing

MATERIALS
Paper and pencil

GROUP SIZE
10–30

TIME
10–20 minutes

OBJECTIVE
Students will design a personal time capsule.

INSTRUCTIONS
1. Discuss the concept of a time capsule with your class. Describe items that could be included in a time capsule such as a teddy bear, photos, books, scrapbooks, and charms.
2. Tell the group that they are going to create their own time capsule that will be buried for two hundred years. (They will not really be doing this; the game is to design the capsule.) The items included in the time capsule should communicate something to the people that find the capsule in two hundred years.
3. Ask everyone to write down all the personal items they would want to include in their time capsule.

VARIATIONS

Limit the number of items that they can include in their personal time capsule.

PROCESSING QUESTIONS

How did you choose the items you put in your time capsule? What is the most important thing you want the world to know about you in the future? What legacy do you wish to pass along to others? If you were to create a personal time capsule twenty years from now, how different would your personal time capsule look?

CHAPTER 5–2ND QUARTER GAMES

MAKING CONNECTIONS

GAME TYPE
Icebreaker; processing

MATERIALS
None

GROUP SIZE
10–30

TIME
10–20 minutes

OBJECTIVES
This is a great but simple way to talk about many topics from bullying, cliques, economic diversity, and cultural diversity. So many times, students don't feel part of a group and can be isolated. This is a safe way for students who may be quiet, or are not part of a group, to see that they have something in common with other kids in their class. As a teacher you can use this game to pair up kids who may not normally get together for activities, labs, and projects.

INSTRUCTIONS
1. Begin this game by saying a trait that you have. For example, "I love pizza," or "I have more than one sibling."

2. Ask everyone that has that same trait to come up to the front of the class and hold hands.
3. You can continue this game by having the last person in the chain state something about themselves with the goal of getting the students still sitting to join the group.
4. The game can also start over from the beginning. Ask everyone to return to their seats and begin again.

VARIATIONS
Create a competition to see who can connect with the most people in one attempt.

PROCESSING QUESTIONS
You can start this game with nonthreatening things such as "I like pizza." Through the course of the year, move to more challenging, harder topics such as:

- I often feel alone.
- I am afraid of the future.
- I am afraid of (fill in the blank).
- I struggle with (fill in the blank).

As the school year progresses and students get more comfortable, you then can push them a little more with rotationally powerful questions that could lead to some very significant growth—not only within individuals, but the group.

ARE YOU MORE LIKE...?

GAME TYPE
Icebreaker; processing

MATERIALS
None

GROUP SIZE
10–40

TIME
5–15 minutes

OBJECTIVES
The simple goal of this game is for the students to see how much they have in common with their classmates.

INSTRUCTIONS
1. Have all of your students stand up and move all the desks to one side.
2. Have the entire class stand in the middle of the room.
3. Start out by asking a question that includes two choices, such as, "Are you more like a sports car or luxury car?"
4. The students must choose and move to one side of the room based on their choice.
5. Repeat this game by offering additional choices.

VARIATIONS

There are countless choice options, such as:

- hamburger/hot dog
- cake/ice cream
- rock music/country music
- action movie/ love story

The list can be geared toward the classroom characteristics and focus on topics such as sports, food, culture, current events, or social and emotional issues.

PROCESSING QUESTIONS

What did you learn through this game? Do you think you are more like your classmates than you believed prior to the game? What differences are surprising?

BACK TO BACK/FACE-TO-FACE

GAME TYPE
Icebreaker; cooperation and communication

MATERIALS
None

GROUP SIZE
10–30

TIME
10–20 minutes

OBJECTIVES
Students will share information about themselves and learn about each other.

INSTRUCTIONS
1. Separate the class into pairs.
2. Ask everyone to stand back to back with their partners.
3. Ask a question such as:

    - What is your favorite meal?
    - What was your scariest moment?
    - What was your favorite vacation?
    - What do you plan to be doing five years from now?

4. After hearing the question, the students face each other and describe their answers.
5. Each student finds another partner, and the game continues.

VARIATIONS

This game can be used to cover a wide range of topics, including some probing and thought-provoking questions.

PROCESSING QUESTIONS

What did you learn about your classmates? What did you learn that was surprising?

TURN AROUND

GAME TYPE
Icebreaker; cooperation and communication

MATERIALS
None

GROUP SIZE
Groups of 3–6 students

TIME
10–20 minutes

OBJECTIVE
This activity will help get the group to work together as a team.

INSTRUCTIONS
1. Ask all students to stand. Divide the classroom into small groups (3–6 per team).
2. Call out a number.
3. On the count of three, all team members hold up fingers (randomly between one and ten fingers).
4. If the total number of fingers equals what the teacher called out, the entire team can sit down.
5. If the group does not match the number the teacher called, they must turn around in their place, based on the number of total fingers thrown by their team. For example, if the teacher called out the number "six" and the

group threw a "ten," all team members must turn around ten times.

6. This game can be repeated as time permits.

VARIATIONS
- After each round, create new teams.
- Keep the teams intact and keep score.
- Record the winning score on the chalkboard for other classes to see or to try to beat at a later date.

PROCESSING QUESTIONS
Were you frustrated when your group could not finish the game the first few times? What are examples of frustrations in your life? How do you deal with frustrations in your life?

BODY SPELLING

GAME TYPE
Icebreaker; cooperation and communication

MATERIALS
None

GROUP SIZE
6–10 per team

TIME
10–30 minutes

OBJECTIVE
The goal of this activity is to have students spell words by using their bodies.

INSTRUCTIONS
1. Organize your class into teams of 6–10 students.
2. Provide a list of words that each team needs to spell with their bodies, or allow each team to choose their own words(warning the students to only choose appropriate words). The words should have the same number of letters as the number of students on each team, so each student can represent one letter.
3. Ask each team to spell their word and ask the rest of the class to guess what the word is.

VARIATIONS

- You can use this activity to incorporate vocabulary words from a lesson, or make them use words from current events (political, social, or entertainment).
- The teams can be assigned a category—such as movies, cartoons, or current events—that they must consider when choosing their words.
- Ask the class to line up and create the entire alphabet with their bodies.

PROCESSING QUESTIONS

How hard was it to put your body in the shape of a letter? What letters were the hardest to shape?

PUSH-UP WRESTLING

GAME TYPE
Icebreaker

MATERIALS
None

GROUP SIZE
Groups of 2

TIME
2–5 minutes

OBJECTIVES
This activity will help students have fun, and will create friendly competition

INSTRUCTIONS
1. Separate the classroom into pairs—matching gender, size, and athletic ability as much as possible.
2. Ask everyone to get into plank position while facing each other.
3. When you give them the signal to go, each student tries to knock their opposing partner down by swiping at his hands or body.

VARIATIONS
- This activity can be done with eyes closed.
- Keep track of champions and have them go against other classes.

PROCESSING QUESTIONS

Did you feel you were evenly paired up with your partner? Have you ever had a competition where there was an unfair advantage? How did you deal with it? Are you competitive? If not, how do you deal with competitive people?

WELDED ANKLES

GAME TYPE
Icebreaker; cooperation and communication

MATERIALS
None

GROUP SIZE
Groups of 2

TIME
10–20 minutes

OBJECTIVES
The objects are to work together as a team, communicate, and have fun.

INSTRUCTIONS
1. Separate the classroom into pairs.
2. Ask each pair to stand next to each other.
3. Tape their ankles together with masking tape.
4. Make an obstacle course in your room, gym, or outside (depending on time/space). An obstacle course can be very simple, or as complex as you want to make it. You can use shoes, erasers, etc. to mark the course. The course could also include walking over desks, etc.
5. Time each group to see which team can get through the course fastest while having "welded" ankles.

VARIATIONS

- Group students based on class grades, gender, rows, or any other way to get students to know each other.
- You can blindfold 1members of each group, or not allow any talking.
- Allow the winning team to setup the course the next time.

PROCESSING QUESTIONS

How did it feel to have to work as one unit? Have you ever been stuck in a group, project, or lab where someone in the group or team was not working together? If so, how did you deal with it? Can you think of other times in your life where you were forced to work with someone that you did not agree with? If so, how did you work it out with them?

SCRAMBLE

GAME TYPE
Icebreaker; cooperation and communication

MATERIALS
Prepare lists of scrambled words

GROUP SIZE
Groups of 2-4

TIME
5-20 minutes

OBJECTIVES
Students will communicate and work with their group to unscramble words.

INSTRUCTIONS
1. Put students in groups of 2-4.
2. Give them scrambled words to unscramble. These can be vocabulary words from a current lesson, unit, the whole semester, current events, or last names of students in your class.
3. Time the teams to see how fast each group can unscramble the words.

VARIATIONS
Have the group come up with a list of their own words (as long as they are appropriate).

PROCESSING QUESTIONS

What was the hardest part of this activity? Do you get nervous in timed events? Are you more of a visual learner or an auditory learner? How do you learn best?

BALLOON DROP

GAME TYPE
Icebreaker; cooperation and communication

MATERIALS
Balloon or beach ball

GROUP SIZE
10–20

TIME
10–30 minutes

OBJECTIVES
The goal of this game is for students to work together as a team.

INSTRUCTIONS
1. Divide the class into two groups.
2. The students can either stand, or line their desks in a random way with one group on one side of the room and the other on the other side of the room.
3. Hold up a balloon or beach ball and tell them that it is full of nitroglycerin. Say that if it ever touches the ground it will explode, and everyone from their group is going to die.
4. Toss the ball to one group first. They have to hit it back to the other group, keeping it in the air.
5. The other group does the same, trying to keep the balloon or beach ball from touching the ground.

6. Keep track of the number of times it touches the ground. Award a point to the other team when it does.
7. Once you are ready, introduce a second balloon to the game, and then a third.

VARIATIONS

- During the game, call out "left hand" or "right hand" before participants hit it each time.
- Only allow them to use their legs to hit the ball. (Have you ever seen students sitting at their desks trying to reach a leg out to hit a balloon in the air? I have, and it is worth it).
- Allow them to only use their heads.
- Go to an open field or gym. Spread the group out over the larger space.

PROCESSING QUESTIONS

If this were truly a life-and-death situation and the balloon would really explode when it was dropped, how would you do this activity differently? Have you ever been in a situation that you thought was life-and-death, such as having to fight someone, or having someone trying to hurt you? If so, how did you deal with that situation?

ELECTRIC CURRENT

GAME TYPE
Icebreaker, cooperation and communication

MATERIALS
None

GROUP SIZE
10–50

TIME
5–15 minutes

OBJECTIVE
Students will work together as a group.

INSTRUCTIONS
1.   Have your students stand up and hold hands to make a giant circle.
2.   Explain to your students how an electric current works. (Electric currents move from one object to the next.)
3.   Ask the students to pretend that they are one giant conductor and they have to pass the electric current around the circle as fast as they can.
4.   Start with one person. When you say "go," he or she squeezes the hand of the person to their right. As soon as the person to their right gets the "current" (hand squeezed), they then squeeze the hand of the person to their right.

5. The "current" gets passed around the entire circle until it comes back to the first person.
6. Time them and see how fast they can pass the current around the circle.

VARIATIONS

- Keep track of the time. Track the best time for the class to beat.
- Compete with other classes and keep a record of how fast they can pass the current.
- As the students to play this game with their eyes closed.

PROCESSING QUESTIONS

What worked with the group? What did not work with the group? Was there a leader of the group? If so, who chose them? Does there always need to be a leader? Have you ever wanted to be a leader, but no one would let you? If so, explain.

AUTO PARTS

GAME TYPE
Icebreaker; cooperation and communication

MATERIALS
None

GROUP SIZE
Groups of 4–8

TIME
5–15 minutes

OBJECTIVES
The objectives of this activity are to have the group work together to create something, and to get your students to talk about how they see themselves.

INSTRUCTIONS
1. Break into groups of 4–8.
2. Tell each group they are to design a car, and that they are each a car part.
3. They must explain how they are like the car part they chose and how it relates to their view on life. For example, a student may choose to be an accelerator because that would allow them to be in charge of how fast they move.
4. Once all the members of the "car" are assembled, they must unite into one "car" and move from a starting point to an ending

point, all the while making the noise of the car they chose.

VARIATIONS
Have car races.

PROCESSING QUESTIONS
Why did you choose the car part you did? How are you like that car part? Do you see that in order for a car to run, it takes many different parts with many different functions—just like life, a sports team, or an
office?

"SIMON SAYS" GROUP-OFF

GAME TYPE
Icebreaker; communication

MATERIALS
None

GROUP SIZE
10–40 people

TIME
10–20 minutes

OBJECTIVES
Students will listen to directions and communicate.

INSTRUCTIONS
1. Divide your class into groups. The groups could be created from rows, boys versus girls, etc.
2. Have the two groups face each other. One group starts off by saying, "Simon says" combined with a direction (such as "lift your left leg").
3. Any members on the opposing team that don't following the direction ("lift your left leg") are out. If no one is out, the other team gets to communicate a direction to the opposing team.
4. The group can try to trick the opposing group by not saying "Simon" first.
5. The winning team is the team with the most people standing after a set amount of time.

Example " Simon Says" directions:

- Lift your left leg.
- Touch your nose with the pinky finger of your right hand.
- Shake your right hand while turning around 360 degrees to the left.
- Put your right hand on your left hip and left hand on your right ear.
- Shake the right hand of the person to your left.

VARIATIONS

Start the game slowly, picking up the pace so that the class has to react quickly to the request or they are out.

PROCESSING QUESTIONS

Do you have a hard time following directions? When have you gotten into trouble by not following directions?

BODY PARTS/PEOPLE TO PEOPLE

GAME TYPE
Icebreaker

MATERIALS
None

GROUP SIZE
9–49—Each group should have an odd number of students

TIME
15–20 minutes

OBJECTIVES
The object of this activity is to help students get to know each other and interact with each other.

INSTRUCTIONS
1. If it is a nice day, go outside, or use the gym.
2. Get your class into a large circle.
3. Start with one person in the middle.
4. The person in the middle names two body parts—for example, right hand to left ear.
5. When he shouts "People to people!" the entire group runs to find someone to connect with—except the people next to them—and places their right hand on that persons left ear (or vice versa).
6. The person left after everyone selects their partner becomes the person in the middle.
7. The game continues with students making a new circle and a new command is given.

8.   Students cannot connect with the same
      person more than one time.

VARIATIONS
Call out more than 2 body parts.

PROCESSING QUESTIONS
Are you uncomfortable having body contact
with other people? If so, why? Is personal space
important to you? If so, how do you handle it
when people violate your "personal space"?

LIAR, LIAR, PANTS ON FIRE

GAME TYPE
Icebreaker

MATERIALS
Paper and pencil for each student

GROUP SIZE
10–20

TIME
10–20 minutes

OBJECTIVES
The object of the activity is to get the students to interact with each other and share fun information about themselves.

INSTRUCTIONS
1. Have your students write down on a piece of paper two things about themselves that are true. These truths can be about how many siblings they have, where they have been on vacation, famous people they have met, or fun things they have tried.
2. On that same piece of paper, have them put one lie. These lies can be simple things such as their middle name, people they have met, or things they are afraid of.
3. Have the students read their three statements out loud one at a time. The class has to guess which ones were true and which one was a lie.

VARIATIONS

Have the students write each individual truth and lie on separate pieces of paper and put them all into a hat. Draw each one out and see if the class can guess whom it belongs to.

PROCESSING QUESTIONS

Have you ever lied to someone about something but were not caught? What was the lie? Why did you lie? What did the person do when they found out you were lying to them? Have you ever been lied to? How did you deal with it?

STRIKE A POSE

GAME TYPE
Icebreaker; communication and cooperation

MATERIALS
None

GROUP SIZE
Groups of 6–10

TIME
10–20 minutes

OBJECTIVES
The goal of the activity is to have the group work together as a team to determine what in the room has changed.

INSTRUCTIONS
1. Divide your class into teams of 6–10.
2. Explain that one group at a time is going to strike a pose, with the entire group standing next to each other. The rest of the class will study the pose of everyone in the group.
3. Students in the group that struck the pose leave the room together, and determine one change that each student will make to their pose. For example, someone can untie a shoelace, put their hand in their pocket, move their watch from one hand to the other, etc. (Remind the students that all changes need to be visible).

4. The group comes back into the room and strikes the new pose.
5. The rest of the class then tries to decide what one thing each member changed. (It is a good idea to limit the number of guesses per person to two.)

VARIATIONS
- Keep track of who guesses each change and award a point to each person that guesses correctly.
- Award a point to the person who changed something that the group could not guess.

PROCESSING QUESTIONS
When you meet someone, do you pay attention to details? What feature about yourself do you want people to pay attention to the most and why?

PETER PIPER

GAME TYPE
Icebreaker

MATERIALS
A nursery rhyme, song, or poem with many words that all start with the same letter, such as "Peter Piper"

GROUP SIZE
10–20

TIME
10–20 minutes

OBJECTIVES
The object of the game is for students to pay attention to details.

INSTRUCTIONS
1.   Ask everyone to stand.
2.   On an overhead or handout, go over the words to a nursery rhyme, song, or poem.
3.   Have the entire class read through the nursery rhyme.
4.   Every time the class says a word that starts with the dominant letter, they alternate squatting and standing. Instruct the class to squat the first time a word is read that starts with the dominant letter, and have them stand on the second time a word is read that starts with the dominant letter.

5. Similar to "Simon Says," if someone is standing up when they are supposed to be squatting, they are out.
6. Begin this game by reading the rhyme slowly, but increase the pace of the game as students start getting comfortable with it.
7. The last person standing wins the game.

PROCESSING QUESTIONS

Were you frustrated as the game got faster and faster? Were you looking around at others for directions, or did you focus on the game and what you had to do?

HAND JIVE

GAME TYPE
Icebreaker; cooperation and communication

MATERIALS
None

GROUP SIZE
5–20

TIME
5–20 minutes

OBJECTIVES
The object of this activity is for students to improve teamwork.

INSTRUCTIONS
Instruct the group to begin stacking their fists on top of each other while their feet are flat on the ground.

VARIATIONS
- Time the group to see how long it takes for each activity. Keep track of records, and mix the groups up.
- Change the activity to stack hands, rather than stack fists.
- Make this a tournament, awarding the championship team.

PROCESSING QUESTIONS

What was the most challenging thing about this activity? Do you have a hard time being in an activity where you were so close physically to people? What is your "personal space" and how do you deal with it when people violate it?

GUESS WHO?

GAME TYPE
Icebreaker

MATERIALS
Paper and pencil

GROUP SIZE
10–25

TIME
10–20 minutes

OBJECTIVES
The goal of this activity is for students to get to know more about their classmates' interests and qualities.

INSTRUCTIONS
1. Ask the students to write their traits, qualities, values, and interests on separate pieces of paper.
2. Once your class has put all these individual traits on a piece of paper, have them fold them and put them into a box.
3. Read one piece of paper at a time and ask the class to guess who wrote down each trait, quality, value, or interest. Limit the guess to three.
4. If no one guesses the trait, ask the student with that trait to raise their hand and award them a small prize or privilege.

VARIATIONS

- You don't need to go over all the qualities in the box at one time. This is an activity that can be spread over several days.
- This can be an activity that lasts all semester. When an individual student thinks of a new trait or quality or interest, they can put it in the box.

PROCESSING QUESTIONS

Were you surprised that a trait belonged to a particular person? Are there things you don't show people? If so, why? What is something you want people to know about you?

QUESTION PROGRESSION

GAME TYPE
Icebreaker; processing

MATERIALS
None

GROUP SIZE
10–20

TIME
10–20 minutes

OBJECTIVES
The object of this activity is to get to know your students better and to allow them to get to know each other better.

INSTRUCTIONS
1.   Start with a series of nonthreatening questions that ,do not require a lot of self-disclosure, such as the following:

   • What is your favorite color?
   • Who is your best friend?
   • What is your favorite food?
   • What is your favorite sports team?
   • What musician or music is your favorite?

2.   Ask random students to raise their hands and answer the questions.
3.   The next set of questions is more personal; for example:

- What are you most proud of?
- Whom do you trust most in life?
- What are you afraid of?
- What stresses you out?
- What makes you happy?

4. The last set of questions is deeper and riskier, such as:

- What was the most embarrassing moment in your life?
- What is your deepest life regret?
- If you could change one thing about yourself, what would it be?

VARIATIONS

You do not have to do this entire activity all at one time. You can try the first set of questions the first week, and gradually add tougher questions. When you are ready for the toughest questions, you may only want to address one question per week as the semester progresses. The answers to the question could create 10–20 minutes of conversation, teaching moments, and opportunities to address emotional topics.

PROCESSING QUESTIONS

Is it hard to share personal information with people? If so, why? What did you learn about your classmates today?

HOW FAST CAN YOU PASS?

GAME TYPE
Icebreaker; cooperation and communication

MATERIALS
Any object you can pass

GROUP SIZE
10–30

TIME
5–15 minutes

OBJECTIVES
The object of this activity is for students to problem solve and learn to work together as a team.

INSTRUCTIONS
1. Have your class or group create a circle.
2. Start by passing large objects around the circle, like a basketball or dodge ball.
3. Time how long it takes to pass the object all the way around the circle.
4. Once the object is passed around the circle, replace it with a smaller object. Continue to switch to smaller objects.

Try using various sizes of balls, books, pencil boxes, erasers, pieces of chalk, etc.

VARIATIONS

- Divide the large group into smaller groups and have them compete against each other.
- Change how the group can pass the object. For example, ask the students to only pass objects behind their backs, between their legs, with their eyes closed, etc.

PROCESSING QUESTIONS

Did you feel your group worked well together? Why or why not? What were your frustrations with your group, if any? How could you have worked better as a group? Did you feel that the team all passed the object the same way?

PICTIONARY CHALLENGE

GAME TYPE
Icebreaker; cooperation and communication

MATERIALS
Index cards

GROUP SIZE
Groups of 4–8

TIME
10–20 minutes

OBJECTIVES
Students will learn to communicate nonverbally while working as a team to achieve a common goal.

INSTRUCTIONS
1. Write the names of famous people, events, movies, current events, or any characters or objects from class (such as elements in science or vocabulary terms) on index cards.
2. Divide your class into groups (boys versus. girls, row versus. row, or create random teams).
3. Have one member of each team come up to the chalkboard and pick a card. Ask that member to act out or draw the object, character, or word on the card. (The words themselves cannot be used in a drawing.)

4. Set a time limit. Ask the first group to guess the character or object on the card. If no one in the first group can guess the answer, ask the second group to guess.
5. Award a point to each group for each one that is correct.

VARIATIONS
- Rank the cards from easiest to hardest, awarding more points for the harder cards.
- Challenge the group to come up with their own list.

PROCESSING QUESTIONS
How could you have communicated better with your group? What was the hardest thing about this activity? Did you feel that communicating without words was hard?

BALLOON RELAYS

GAME TYPE
Icebreaker; cooperation and communication

MATERIALS
Balloons

GROUP SIZE
4-10

TIME
10-20 minutes

OBJECTIVES
Students will work as a team to achieve a common goal.

INSTRUCTIONS
1. Divide the class into groups of 4-10.
2. Identify a starting line and a finish line.
3. A pair from each team must transport a balloon from the starting line to the finish line and back without using their hands.
4. When the pair returns to the starting line, they pass the balloon to the next pair.
5. If the balloon hits the floor, the pair must start the game over.

VARIATIONS
- Try the game with a different size of balloons.
- Make a rule that no 2 pairs on the same team can pass the balloon the same way

(for example, back to back, hip to hip, neck to neck).

- Make an obstacle course students have to go around.

PROCESSING QUESTIONS

How did it feel to not be able to use your hands?

HIGH/LOW

GAME TYPE
Icebreaker; cooperation and communication

MATERIALS
None

GROUP SIZE
10–20

TIME
10–20 minutes

OBJECTIVES
The object is to get students to share the high and lows of their weekend. This is a simple activity for Monday mornings that will help you understand the students' emotions for the week.

INSTRUCTIONS
1. When your students arrive on Monday morning, ask them if any of them would like to share a high or low of their weekend.
2. A high could be that they got to see their favorite movie; a low may be that they got grounded for fighting with their sister.
3. Set a target of 3–4 students to volunteer a high or a low.
4. Keep track of students that are willing to share, and encourage others to speak.

VARIATIONS

- Randomly pick student names to share their high or low.
- Ask students to turn their desks to the right, left, or behind, and simply share with that one person next to them.

PROCESSING QUESTIONS

How did you handle your low? How did you handle your high? What can you do next time so you don't repeat the same "low" next weekend? What part of the "low" or "high" was your responsibility?

PARTNERS FOR LIFE

GAME TYPE
Icebreaker; processing; communication and cooperation

MATERIALS
Chalk, paper, note cards

GROUP SIZE
10–30

TIME
10–20 minutes

OBJECTIVES
Students will be able to communicate using descriptions and characteristics.

INSTRUCTIONS
1. Talk to the class about famous or infamous partners (Bonnie/Clyde, Tonto/Long Ranger, Elmer Fudd/Bugs Bunny, etc.).
2. Have the class come up with as many partners as they can. List them on the board.
3. Write each individual name (not the partners) on a note card or piece of paper.
4. Hand one card to each student randomly. Make sure that each matching partner is included in the deck that is distributed to the class.
5. Ask your students to walk around the room, introducing themselves to other students by describing themselves (and not using their

name). For example, if they are trying to describe Superman, they can say, "I wear a red cape and I was born on another planet."

6.   Go find your partner match.

VARIATIONS

- Come up with your own list of partners and do not share them with the class. These partners can be history figures (Lewis/Clark), Obama/Biden), sports figures (Jordan/Pippen), or any other pairs you find interesting.
- Do not let your students talk at all. They can only communicate who they are by acting them out.

PROCESSING QUESTIONS

If you could pick one famous pair to be a part of, who would it be and why? Which partner would you not want to be, and why? Do you have a partner in your life? Who is it? Describe your partnership.

CHAPTER 6–3RD QUARTER GAMES

ALL IN

GAME TYPE
Icebreaker; cooperation and communication; problem solving

MATERIALS
There are no special materials required for this game. Any classroom objects will work well. Choose objects and sort them from largest to smallest—for example: desk, book, eraser, and quarter.

GROUP SIZE
Groups of 4–6

TIME
10–20 minutes

OBJECTIVES
The object of this game is to have the group learn to work together, problem solve, and achieve a common goal.

INSTRUCTIONS
1. Put your students into groups of 4–6.
2. Put an object on the floor. Start off with the largest item.

3. Instruct the students that every person in the group must touch the first object with any body part.
4. Add an item to the game. Make sure it is smaller than the last item.
5. Repeat this with several more objects, adding smaller objects each time.
6. As each object is added, students must continue their contact with all prior objects.

VARIATIONS

- You can modify this activity based on the students' skill level and their ability to work together and communicate.
- You can have the group compete against each other and keep track of which group works the best together.
- Mix teams up at random.

PROCESSING QUESTIONS

How did you feel being so close to each other? Did you feel you could not achieve the goal at any given point? Were you frustrated at any point? When and how did you work through it? Have you ever felt like this outside of the classroom? If so, how did you get through it?

LAP SIT

GAME TYPE
Trust; problem solving; cooperation and communication

MATERIALS
None

GROUP SIZE
10–50

TIME
10–20 minutes

OBJECTIVES
The group will all sit down on each other's laps and not fall over.

INSTRUCTIONS
1. Ask the group to gather into a tight circle.
2. Ask everyone to turn sideways.
3. On your count, ask all the students to sit down at the same time—without falling over.

VARIATIONS
- Break the group into smaller groups.
- Try this with all the students in the class.
- Lap Lie is a tougher version of the Lap Sit.

PROCESSING QUESTIONS
How did it feel to have to count on the person in front of you and behind you to do this without falling? How did it feel to be so close to someone

(on your lap)? How do you handle awkward moments like this in your life? Did you trust the person behind you to be there for you? Have people let you down before when you trusted them? How did that feel? How did you deal with it?

HUMAN KNOT

GAME TYPE
Icebreaker; cooperation and communication; problem solving

MATERIALS
None

GROUP SIZE
Groups of 6–10

TIME
10–20 minutes

OBJECTIVES
The objective of this game is to get the group to undo the knot. The team must work together to solve the problem and communicate.

INSTRUCTIONS
1. Organize the class into groups of 6–10.
2. Ask the students to place their right hand in the circle and grab the hand of someone who is not next to them.
3. Next, ask the students to place their left hand in the circle and grab the hand of someone hand who is not next to them (and is not the same person with whom they are linking their right hand).
4. Ask the class to undo the knot without letting go of the hands they are holding. If they do break hands, have them start all over again.

VARIATIONS

- Time each group to see who has the fastest time. Keep track of the record on a chalkboard. See if that time can be broken, either by your class or another group.
- Ask the students to accomplish undoing the knot without verbal communication.
- Only allow one person to talk. (Consider choosing a quiet student who is not used to being the leader.)

PROCESSING QUESTIONS

How did it feel to lose your voices and have to communicate without words? Were you comfortable being so close to other people? If not, how did you handle it? Did you feel like your voice was heard and your group was listening to you? How did it feel when your group was struggling? Have you struggled in groups before? If so, how did you resolve it?

FIRE IN THE HOLE

GAME TYPE
Trust; icebreaker; cooperation and communication

MATERIALS
None

GROUP SIZE
Groups of 6–12

TIME
10–20 minutes

OBJECTIVES
The object of this game is for students to work together and to communicate.

INSTRUCTIONS
1. Divide your class into groups of 6–12.
2. Have two members from the group make a circle with their arms.
3. The rest of the team must get through the hole without touching any part of the circle made by their teammates. If they touch, they must start over.
4. The first team that gets all their team members through wins.

VARIATIONS
- You can split teams by row, gender, or any other logical ways.

- A fun twist is to blindfold the members going through circle—allowing only the students making the circle to communicate.

PROCESSING QUESTIONS

Did your group work well together? If not, why? What did you do to help out your team?

ROCK, PAPER, SCISSORS

GAME TYPE
Icebreaker; cooperation and communication

MATERIALS
None

GROUP SIZE
10–50

TIME
10–20 minutes

OBJECTIVES
The object is for each team to get as many opposing team members on their side as they can, within a defined time period.

INSTRUCTIONS
1. Have your class organize into two groups facing each other in pairs.
2. On the count of three, shout out, "Rocks, papers, scissors, go!"
3. On "go," each student "throws" rock, paper, or scissors with the person across from them.
4. The losing student must join the side of the winning person.

VARIATIONS
If you are able to go outside or into the gym you can change the game so each team as a *whole* decides which object they want to throw (rock, paper, or scissors). When you come to the line

across from the other team, the same thing happens; everyone throws rock, paper, or scissors at the same time as decided by the team. The winning team then tags as many of the opposing team members as possible. (Establish a safety line that the losing team members need to run past in order to be safe). After each round, each team gets together to decide what to throw. The game continues until one team has everyone from the opposing side on their team, or until the time runs out.

PROCESSING QUESTIONS

Did you feel the team was equally divided up? How do you handle situations where things are not fair?

CHICKEN OR EGG; HAWK OR EAGLE

GAME TYPE
Processing questions; icebreaker, and communication

MATERIALS
None

GROUP SIZE
10–40

TIME
10–20 minutes

OBJECTIVES
The object of the game is for students to become "eagles" and be on top of the food chain.

INSTRUCTIONS
1. Start the game by having the entire class squat on the ground like an egg. Explain to the class that all chickens start off as eggs, all eggs want grow up to get to be chickens, all chickens wish they were hawks, and all hawks wish they were eagles (because they are at the top of the food chain).
2. Everyone starts out as an egg (squatting).
3. Each student pairs with another student (egg) while still squatting.
4. On the count of three, each student throws rock, paper, or scissors.
5. The winning student becomes a chicken and has to find another chicken (still squatting)

to throw "rock, paper, scissors" with in hopes of becoming a hawk.

6. Losing students need to find another egg to play against.
7. Students winning the second round become hawks and get to stand. Hawks play against hawks with the ultimate goal of becoming eagles. The eagle gets to soar around the room watching the rest of the class of eggs, chickens, and hawks continue their competition.
8. Set a time limit to end the game and process afterward.

VARIATIONS

You can have awards for those who make it to become eagles, or allow them to have special privileges.

PROCESSING QUESTIONS

How did it feel to be stuck as an egg? (There will be certain students that can't seem to move past the egg stage) Eagles, how did it feel to be on top of the food chain? Did you feel better or more powerful than the others? How in life have we felt below or above others? How do we handle it when someone thinks they are better than us? What do you need to feel powerful? Have you ever felt excluded out of a group or club, like an egg among eagles?

BARNYARD

GAME TYPE
Trust; icebreaker; cooperation and communication

MATERIALS
None

GROUP SIZE
10–50

TIME
10–20 minutes

OBJECTIVES
The objective is for the class to work as a team and have fun.

INSTRUCTIONS
1. Organize your class into 2–4 groups.
2. Assign each group an animal—for example, pig or cow.
3. Once you have assigned each group and animal, ask everyone to scatter around the room, gym, or outside.
4. Instruct them to close their eyes and try to find their group *only* by making the noise their animal makes.
5. The first team to get all their members together wins.

VARIATIONS

- Give an award for the best-sounding group.
- Put together more than one category of animal sounds.

PROCESSING QUESTIONS

How did you feel having to close your eyes and finding your group by sound only?

What animals made the best noise? If you were to be an animal, what animal would it be and why?

MY PROBLEMS ARE YOUR PROBLEMS NOW

GAME TYPE
Processing questions; cooperation and trust

MATERIALS
Pen and paper

GROUP SIZE
10–20

TIME
15–30 minutes

OBJECTIVES
The objective of this game is to help students understand that they are not alone in their problems. There are solutions to problems that are sometimes not obvious, but other people may have a solution. By playing this game, students learn to be open to other people.

INSTRUCTIONS
1. Explain to the class that everyone in life has problems, including teachers, doctors, professional athletes, and actors. Sometimes our problems seem unsolvable and it's impossible to see the solutions. Talking to other people can help us find other options to solving our own problems that we did not think of ourselves. Problems can include something that is currently happening in their

lives, something that happened a while ago, or something that they are worried about in the future.

2. Ask the students to put their desks in a circle if possible, so everyone can be face-to-face. Students can also remain in rows if moving is not feasible.

3. Ask the students to each write down a problem they have had in the past, or are currently facing, on a piece of paper. Have them pass their problem to the person behind them.

4. The student that receives the problem then writes on the sheet of paper how he or she would deal with that problem.

5. Continue passing the problem around the room and having students write down their solutions until the paper gets back to the original student.

6. At the end, each student has list of solutions from their classmates.

VARIATIONS

- Ask the students to come to class with a fictional problem, or you can make up a fictional problem. Talk about how they would solve that problem.
- Use a real-world problem (from world news, community problems, etc.). Talk about how students would resolve that problem.

PROCESSING QUESTIONS

Was it hard to talk about your problems with other people? Did you feel like you would be judged? What did you think of the suggestions from your peers? How do you feel about helping others with their problems? Who do you usually go to when you have problems? Are you open to other people's ideas? If not, why?

PARTNER TAG

GAME TYPE
Icebreaker; communication and cooperation

MATERIALS
None

GROUP SIZE
10–20

TIME
10–20 minutes

OBJECTIVES
The object is for the group to capture all the group members while working as a team.

INSTRUCTIONS
1. If possible, take the class to the gym or an outside field.
2. Create teams of 2 students and establish a boundary.
3. Have each student link arms at their elbows with their partner.
4. Assign one pair as the tagging team, or "It."
5. Once you say "go," the "It" pair needs to run around (while arms are still linked) and try to tag the other pairs whose arms are also linked. All teams need to stay within the defined boundaries.
6. When the "It" team tags another team, they all link arms and continue to chase the other pairs.

7.	The chase continues, and every group that is captured links arms as one giant team, trying to tag every pair and having them join their ever-expanding team.
8.	The game ends when there is only one group left.

VARIATIONS
- Make the boundaries bigger as more people are added to the "It" group.
- Put a time limit on the game.
- If a group unlocks arms or goes out of bounds, they are automatically on the "It" team.

PROCESSING QUESTIONS
Was it harder to work in pairs or in a team? Do you prefer working alone or in a team? Why?

WHO AM I? WHO ARE YOU?

GAME TYPE
Icebreaker; problem solving

MATERIALS
None

GROUP SIZE
Individual or groups of 2–6

TIME
10–30 minutes

OBJECTIVES
This activity can be used as a review of people the students have studied in class, or as a fun activity that gets the class engaged in discussions and role-playing.

INSTRUCTIONS
1. Secretly assign each student or small group a character. This character can be someone you have been studying, someone in the news, an entertainer, or a sports figure. You can also let the students pick their own character; suggest they choose someone everyone would know.
2. Ask one student at a time to come up in front of the class and give small bits of information about their character.
3. Award a point to the person or groups who guess the character first.

VARIATIONS

- Make this activity a competition. Keep track of the group or individuals who get the character right.
- You can play this game over a number of days. You can have just one group play each day, and the other groups or individuals can take their turns over the course of the next few days or weeks.
- You could play this game based on a theme which can vary each week, such as sports, entertainers, history, scientists, etc.

PROCESSING QUESTIONS

What characters did you enjoy playing the best? Do you ever act like a character other than yourself when you are around other people?

A PICTURE SAYS A THOUSAND WORDS

GAME TYPE
Icebreaker; cooperation and communication

MATERIALS
Pictures from old magazines or books

GROUP SIZE
10–20

TIME
10–20 minutes

OBJECTIVES
Students will try to interpret facial expressions and body language while telling a story.

INSTRUCTIONS
1. Cut out pictures from the local paper, magazines, etc.
2. Put all the pictures in a bowl and ask students to come up and choose a picture.
3. Ask the students to create a story about the picture. Each story needs to be more than one sentence. Encourage the students to have fun with their stories and to be creative.
4. Once they tell their story, you tell the class the real story behind the picture and see how closely their story matched the real story.

VARIATIONS

- A great variation to this activity is to lay out all the pictures, and ask one student at a time

  to develop a story—moving from one picture to the next (as the story moves from one student to the next).
- Divide the class into small groups and give them a set of pictures asking the group to develop a story.

PROCESSING QUESTIONS

One of the most important processing pieces in this activity is that we often judge people and situations without knowing the true story. The old saying "you can't judge a book by its cover" can be used as a way to process bullying, cultural differences, physical appearances, social differences, etc. Have you judged people without having much information about them? Have you ever been judged? If so, how did it feel? What do you do if you feel that someone is judging someone else?

THERE'S A SHARK IN THE WATER

GAME TYPE
Icebreaker; trust; cooperation and communication

MATERIALS
Tarp (size can vary)

GROUP SIZE
10–20

TIME
10–20 minutes

OBJECTIVES
The objective of this game is to encourage the class to work together as a team, learn trust, and communicate with each other.

INSTRUCTIONS
1. Lay a tarp on the floor of your classroom (the size of the tarp is up to you).
2. Have all your students stand on the tarp.
3. Tell them the tarp represents a raft. They are in the ocean, and all around are sharks.
4. They must flip the tarp completely over, while not stepping off the tarp and putting their toes in the water around them. If they step off the tarp, they have to start all over.

VARIATIONS
- If the tarp is too big and it's too easy to flip, fold it in half and have them start again.

- Take away all the voices of the group, or limit who can talk. Sometimes one or two persons take over a group and the quieter ones are not heard. Give them a voice.

PROCESSING QUESTIONS

How did it feel when you kept stepping off the tarp and had to start over? Did you feel like your teammates were listening to you? If not, how did that make you feel? Have you ever felt like you were not listened to? When? What did you do? Did you feel like the group worked well together as a unit?

JUMP ROPE PASS-THROUGH

GAME TYPE
Icebreaker; cooperation and communication; trust

MATERIALS
Jump rope

GROUP SIZE
10–20

TIME
10–20 minutes

OBJECTIVES
Students will work together as a group.

INSTRUCTIONS
1. Have your entire class run through a rope that is being twirled, without stopping the rope.
2. If the rope gets stopped, the class needs to start over.

VARIATIONS
* Using a large rope, try to see how many students can jump rope at the same time. Add 1 person at a time. Keep track of how many students can jump at once.

PROCESSING QUESTIONS
What is the hardest thing about working with a group in order to achieve a common goal? Were you a leader in this activity?

JUMP ROPE WIGGLE

GAME TYPE
Icebreaker; cooperation and communication; trust

MATERIALS
Jump rope

GROUP SIZE
10–20

TIME
10–20 minutes

OBJECTIVE
Students will work together as a group.

INSTRUCTIONS
1. Start the jump rope on the ground with the people at both ends moving it back and forth so it looks like a snake.
2. Tell the students that the rope is a poisonous snake, and they must get over it without touching it or they will be stung.
3. As the entire class passes over the slithering rope, ask the students shaking the rope to raise it up a few inches. Ask the class try again to get over the shaking rope without it touching them.
4. If someone touches the rope, the game starts over with the rope on the ground.

5. Continue raising the rope as the students gets past each level. Measure how high the rope gets.

PROCESSING QUESTIONS
What is the hardest thing about working with a group in order to achieve a common goal? Were you a leader in this activity?

ROPE KNOT

GAME TYPE
Icebreaker; cooperation and communication; trust

MATERIALS
Jump rope

GROUP SIZE
10–20

TIME
10–20 minutes

OBJECTIVE
Students will work together as a group.

INSTRUCTIONS
1. Tie knots in a long rope.
2. Have the entire group hold the rope with only one hand.
3. Ask the group to undo the knots without letting go of the rope.
4. The group can slide their hands up and down the knot, but cannot let go of the rope or use their other hand.

PROCESSING QUESTIONS
What is the hardest thing about working with a group in order to achieve a common goal? Were you a leader in this activity?

HUMAN OBSTACLE COURSE

GAME TYPE
Trust; processing questions; communication and cooperation

MATERIALS
Any object that you want to be part of your obstacle course

GROUP SIZE
10–20

TIME
15–45 minutes

OBJECTIVES
The objective of this game is to increase trust, teamwork, and communication among students.

INSTRUCTIONS
1. Take your class to a large open space, such as a gym or outside field.
2. Divide the class into pairs.
3. One pair will take a turn at a time going through a human obstacle course formed by the rest of the class.
4. The obstacles will be made entirely from their bodies. For example, one pair of students might make a bridge from their hands that other students will go under, or linked their hands in a way that other students will walk over.

5. One student from each pair will close their eyes. The other student will be responsible for giving commands to their partner.
6. After the student has safely guided his or her partner through the human obstacle course, they switch roles.
7. After each pair has completed the task, another group will attempt the same task.

VARIATIONS

- You can time each group and keep track of the fastest group.
- If someone going through the course touches one of the obstacles, they need to start the entire course over.

PROCESSING QUESTIONS

How did it feel not to be able to see? How did it feel to have to trust someone with verbal commands only? Is trust hard for you? If so, why? How did it feel to watch others go through the course? Did you want to help them? How do you think people who are really blind feel about having to navigate their world without seeing?

STRESS? WHAT STRESS?

GAME TYPE
Icebreaker; problem solving; cooperation and communication

MATERIALS
Paper and pen

GROUP SIZE
Groups of 4–8

TIME
20–45 minutes

OBJECTIVES
The objective is for students to vocalize, reflect on, and laugh at the stress we all have in our lives.

INSTRUCTIONS
1. Divide your class into groups of 4–8.
2. Ask the students to write down a list of things in their lives that create stress.
3. Ask the group to make up a funny story that weaves all their stress elements together into one story.
4. Ask the students to turn their story into a short play that they will perform in front of the class.

VARIATIONS
Give examples of stressful situations. Ask each group to come up with a way to work through that stressful scenario.

PROCESSING QUESTIONS

Did you find that you had stress factors in common with others in your group or other groups? Did you find new ways to deal with your stress factors from other members of your group or other groups? What stress factors do you still struggle with? Why? When you feel stressed, how do you handle it? What are your emotions or methods to deal with your stress?

PUZZLE NEGOTIATIONS

GAME TYPE
Cooperation and communication; problem solving

MATERIALS
Children's puzzles (3–6 with not more than 25 pieces each)

GROUP SIZE
Groups of 4–6

TIME
20–40 minutes

OBJECTIVES
The objective of this game is to work together to complete a puzzle, and to learn to negotiate.

INSTRUCTIONS
1. Place the puzzle pieces from 3–6 simple children's puzzles into a large container.
2. Divide the class into groups of 4–6.
3. Give each group an equal number of puzzle pieces.
4. Tell the groups they have 20 minutes to negotiate with the other groups to get the pieces that fit their puzzle.
5. When the time is up, the team with the most completed puzzle wins.

VARIATIONS

- Create an individual competition to see which member of each group gets the most pieces for their team.
- Allow two groups to form an alliance and work together.

PROCESSING QUESTIONS

How did your negotiations with other teams go? What were some of your frustrations with the other group? What were some of your frustrations with members of your own team? How do you handle it when people you are working with are not acting reasonably? What strategy did you find worked best in order to get what you wanted?

TIMELINE OF CHALLENGES

GAME TYPE
Processing questions; icebreaker; communication

MATERIALS
Paper and pen

GROUP SIZE
10–20

TIME
10–20 minutes

OBJECTIVES
The objective of this game is for students to share information about their lives.

INSTRUCTIONS
1. Ask your students to make a timeline on a piece of paper that represents their life.
2. Ask the students to list events in their lives when they struggled. These struggles can be emotional, physical, academic, social, medical, etc.
3. Ask them to put the events in order from earliest to most recent.
4. When all the timelines are done, ask the students to come up to the front of the class and present their timelines with as much detail as they are comfortable sharing.

PROCESSING QUESTIONS

When you look back on some of the things you've struggled with early in your life, do you see yourself dealing with them differently today? If so, how? What are some of the struggles that have taught you the most? What did you learn about yourself and your ability to deal with tough times in your life? What strategies for dealing with your struggles have worked the best? The worst? Why? Did you learn anything about how your peers deal with their struggles? Can you apply it to how you deal with yours? Were there common things your classmates/peers struggled with? Were you surprised? Do you think you have gotten better at dealing with tough times in your life? Who do you turn to when you are struggling and need help?

MAKE A WISH

GAME TYPE
Problem solving; communication

MATERIALS
Paper and pen; construction paper and markers optional

GROUP SIZE
10–20

TIME
10–20 minutes

OBJECTIVES
The objective of this game is for students to discuss their wishes.

INSTRUCTIONS
1. Talk to your class about wishes. Ask the students to share a single wish that is attainable. It can be a wish for someone else or for themselves.
2. Ask the students to decorate a piece of paper with their wish. They can use construction paper and markers, if available. Ask them to be creative.
3. Once the "make a wish" statements are completed, ask each student to come to the front of the class and explain their wish. Each student can then post their wish on the walls of the classroom.

4. If any of the wishes come true (over time), take them off the wall and ask the students to share their experiences with the class. They can put them on their desks or take them home.

VARIATIONS

Ask each student to create a wish for themselves and one wish for someone else.

PROCESSING QUESTIONS

Why did you choose your wish? Have you always had this wish? If not, what motivated you to choose it? Are your wishes more about you or other people? When you see tragedies on television or in the newspaper like hurricanes or floods, do you want to help? What could you do to help?

LOOKING FOR...?

GAME TYPE
Icebreaker; problem solving; trust

MATERIALS
Paper and pen for each student

GROUP SIZE
10–25

TIME
10–20 minutes

OBJECTIVES
The objective is for students to share information about their lives.

INSTRUCTIONS
1. Read an example of a personal advertisement in the newspaper.
2. Ask your students to write their own personal advertisement. This can include a physical description, interests, a description of their personality, and what they are seeking. Make sure they do not put their names on their personal advertisement.
3. Put all the ads in a container and read them one at a time. Ask the students to match each ad to a student in class.

VARIATIONS
After reading the personal ads, decide who best matches your interests and personality.

PROCESSING QUESTIONS

Do you think what you are looking for now will change in the future? If so, how? Were you surprised about your peers and their interests? Did you discover someone that has the same interests as you?

THE BUCKET LIST

GAME TYPE
Icebreaker; trust; communication; problem solving

MATERIALS
Paper and pen for each student

GROUP SIZE
10–30

TIME
10–20 minutes

OBJECTIVES
The objective is for students to set goals of things they want to do in the future and outline the things necessary to achieve those goals.

INSTRUCTIONS
1. Describe a "bucket list "to your class. (Tell them that this is a list that people sometimes make of things that they want to do before they die.)
2. Ask the students to create their own bucket lists. They can break down the list into things they want to do by certain milestones (the end of the year, within 5 years, within 20 years).
3. For each item, ask them to specify:
   - What will it take for me to achieve this?
   - What must I give up to achieve this?
   - Who will I do these things with?

VARIATIONS

Ask the students to gather their parents' bucket lists. The students should ask their parents if their dreams have changed since they had children. They should also find out which goals their parents have completed, and what is left to achieve.

PROCESSING QUESTIONS

What motivated you to choose the bucket-list activities? Which bucket-list activities do you feel are achievable? Which bucket list activities do you feel you may not reach? Why? Are you willing to do what it takes to achieve your goals? Do you think this list will change in the future? If so, why?

X/O PUZZLE

GAME TYPE
Icebreaker; cooperation and communication

MATERIALS
15 Xs and 15 Os to put on the floor

GROUP SIZE
10–20

TIME
10–40 minutes

OBJECTIVES
The objective is for students to pay attention to details and work together as a team.

INSTRUCTIONS
1. On pieces of Xerox paper or construction paper, make 15 Xs and 15 Os. Put them on the floor 5 across with 6 rows alternating Xs and Os. (See the handout on the next page.)
2. Line your class up around the Xs and Os on the floor.
3. Explain to the class that their goal is to figure out the puzzle, starting at the beginning and ending at the end point.
4. You will create a master key of the pattern that you choose. Only you can see. (It's helpful to use an index card.)
5. Instruct the students that they can step any direction: forward, sideways, diagonal, or backward.

6. If they land on the correct pattern, they can continue. If they make a mistake, you can ring a bell, make a noise, or just say "no."
7. The next person in line then starts at the beginning, retracing the correct steps of the person before them and trying to add steps to complete the entire puzzle.
8. If the next person makes a mistake, the next in line continues, and so on.
9. Once a student solves the pattern, the entire group needs to copy the pattern.
10. There can be *no* verbal commands from the group. (This is where it gets fun, as there is always one student not paying attention.)
11. Change the patterns each time you play the game.

VARIATIONS

- Compete with other classes for time.
- Have multiple sets of Xs and Os, and have smaller groups compete with each other.

PROCESSING QUESTIONS

How did it feel when there were certain members in your group that were not paying attention to the people before them, and you had to keep starting over?

Sample X/O Answer Sheet

Finish

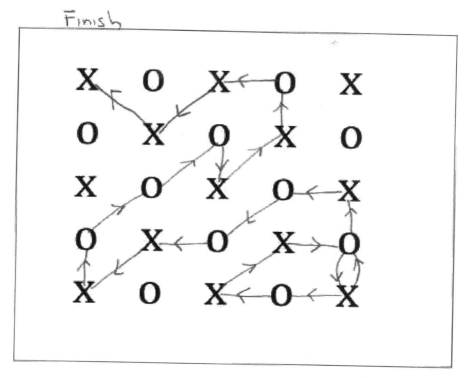

Start

PIN THE TAIL ON ME

GAME TYPE
Icebreaker; cooperation and communication

MATERIALS
Sticky pads, note cards, pens

GROUP SIZE
Groups of 4–8

TIME
10–20 minutes

OBJECTIVES
The objective is for students to learn to communicate using descriptive words.

INSTRUCTIONS
1. Ask your students to write on note cards or sticky pads 3 things about themselves. Each item should be written on a separate piece of paper. For example, a student might write, "Once when I was on vacation, I held a baby alligator," or "I broke my arm falling out of a tree."
2. Once they have written down their 3 experiences, ask the students to put them in a pile.
3. Each student comes up and picks 3 pieces of paper. If someone picks their own, they should choose another.
4. Ask the students to walk around the room interviewing other classmates. They should

try to find the students who wrote the questions they drew. They can ask any question, but cannot use the words on the papers. For example, they can ask, "Have you ever been on a trip where you carried a scary animal?"

5.   The goal is to find the person who matches each card. If you match a person to their card, stick the note to their shirt. The student that finds all 3 matches first wins the game.

VARIATIONS

* Work as teams to see who can come up with the most in a given time.
* Once a group has all their experiences stuck to their shirts, they must come up with a giant story weaving together all their experiences.

PROCESSING QUESTIONS

Were you surprised at some of the experiences that your classmates had? Did you have some of the same experiences as some of your classmates?

ART COOPERATION

GAME TYPE
Icebreaker; cooperation and communication; problem solving

MATERIALS
Paper and crayons (or markers or colored pencils)

GROUP SIZE
Groups of 4–8

TIME
10–20 minutes

OBJECTIVES
The objective of this game is for students to work together as a group to create art and a story.

INSTRUCTIONS
1. Put the class into groups of 4–8.
2. Ask each member of the group to use a different color of crayon.
3. One person in group starts to draw a picture. After a minute or so, yell, "Switch."
4. The next person in the group then adds to the picture.
5. Continue this process until everyone has had a chance to add to the picture.
6. When the groups are all done, ask them to come to the front of the class and have them tell a story about their picture.

VARIATIONS

- When you yell "switch," students have to go to another group and contribute to their picture.
- After all the pictures are done, ask one group to make up a story about other groups' pictures.

PROCESSING QUESTIONS

What was it like to work together with your group to complete the picture? Did you have a different vision for the picture? If so, was it frustrating when the picture kept changing? Do you have an easier time working with other people or by yourself? Why do you think it is important to work with other people?

CHAPTER 7—4TH QUARTER GAMES

GETTING AHEAD IN LIFE

GAME TYPE
Trust; cooperation and communication

MATERIALS
None

GROUP SIZE
10–30

TIME
15–30 minutes

OBJECTIVES
This is a *very* powerful and sometimes emotional game that can really make your students look at their lives,, and the things they control and don't control.

INSTRUCTIONS
1. You will start by telling your students that everyone is born the same—innocent and helpless. There are things in everyone's life that are not controllable that have been positive or negative. For example, if you were born a minority, you may not have the same opportunities that a nonminority may have. If your parents are divorced, or your family only has one income, that can impact your

life. Conversely, some people are born in certain families and are automatically ahead in life.

2.   Continue by exploring things that occur later in life can be controlled and changed.

3.   The goal of this activity is to have your students understand that there are things that they do not control (which can be positive or negative). There are also things that they can control which can also be positive and negative. For example, they can choose to study, abstain from using illegal substances, or choose to participate in a gang.

4.   Begin by asking the students to create a list of things they cannot control that have impacted their lives—both positively and negatively.

5.   Then ask them to create a list of things they can control.

6.   After they are done with their lists, ask the students to line up on a line that you have placed on the floor prior to the activity.

7.   Ask the class a question and tell them to take a step forward or backward depending on the answer. (See the next page for examples.) Be aware that some students may get upset with this activity and not like it.

VARIATIONS

There are so many variables in this activity. You can gear it toward gender issues, race issues, cultures, and age levels. You create the list of questions for the group that you are working with. These questions that you create can be used to address the issues that your group may be dealing with. At the end of the game you can break off into groups to discuss things such as frustrations in their own lives, family, situations they got themselves into, etc.

PROCESSING QUESTIONS

When the game first started out, where were you? Were you ahead of or behind the others? How did it make you feel to be ahead or behind without having done anything in your life yet? What are some of the things that you can control that can help you to move ahead in life? Do you feel like others who were born into other situations have unfair advantages? How does that make you feel? Do you understand that there are many things in life that you do control that can help you out in life? What would you change in your life today to move forward? What are some things that are currently moving you backward that you can change?

SAMPLE QUESTIONS FOR "STEPPING BACK"

- If you are a woman
- If you are a person of color
- If you are a woman of color
- If speaking English is a second language
- If you live in a big city
- If you come from a single parent home
- If you went to one or more elementary schools
- If you live in an apartment
- If you are a non-Christian
- If you have a physical disability
- If you have a learning disability

- If your parents did not go to college
- If you have been to a party where there were drugs or alcohol
- If you have gotten in trouble at school

SAMPLE QUESTIONS FOR "STEPPING FORWARD"

- If you are a male
- If you are white
- If you are a white male
- If you are a Catholic
- If one or both of your parents went to college
- If English is your primary language
- If you never cut a class
- If your homework is always turned in on time
- If your parents are married
- If you live in a house
- If you always try your hardest

BLIND TRUST WALK

GAME TYPE
Trust; problem solving; cooperation and communication

MATERIALS
None

GROUP SIZE
Groups of pairs

TIME
20–40 minutes

OBJECTIVES
The objective is for students to develop trust, and to communicate with someone responsible for their safety.

INSTRUCTIONS
1. Divide the classroom into pairs. Each student can either pick their partner or you can assign them. You may want to assign pairs that don't know each other, or you could just do a random draw.
2. Once everyone is with their partner, you need to explain to the class that this is a trust activity and each student must trust and listen to their partner's directions. If at any time they don't feel safe, they need to tell their partner what they need (i.e., "Stop," or "Slow down and explain that again").

3.	One person in each pair will be blindfolded first. If you don't have blindfolds, the students can just close their eyes.
4.	Once they decide who is going to be "blind" first, you can let them practice.
5.	Ask the "seeing" partner to lead their blind partner around the room, trying to avoid bumping into other people or objects, by giving verbal commands. Give them 10 minutes to practice, and then ask the partners to switch.
6.	After the pair has learned to navigate the room, they can venture outside the class to the hallway, up or down stairs, and around the building. As the facilitator, you really need to stress the importance of safety, trust, and communication.

VARIATIONS

- Take your class outside and have them navigate around the school.
- Switch partners and see if the experience is different.

PROCESSING QUESTIONS

How did it feel to be blind? Did you trust your partner? What was the scariest thing about the activity? How did it feel to be the "eyes"? Do you have a hard time with trust? Why? How do you think people who are really blind handle their disabilities? How do you think individuals such as people who are paralyzed deal with their disabilities? What can you do in your life to be more aware of those who are different from you? What type of disability would be the hardest for you?

MINE WHERE YOU STEP

GAME TYPE
Trust; cooperation and communication; problem solving

MATERIALS
Any objects that you choose to use as a "mine"

GROUP SIZE
10–20

TIME
10–30 minutes

OBJECTIVES
The objective of this trust activity is for students to help their partners navigate through the "minefield" to the finish line without stepping on the "mine," by using only verbal communications. This task can be very difficult because the other teams are also trying to get to the finish line and will be shouting out their commands to their own partners at the same time.

INSTRUCTIONS
1. Find a clear space—a gym, hallway, or outside (ideal).
2. Divide the class into pairs.
3. Setup a "minefield." A mine can be anything from pieces of paper, shoes, books, or backpacks—any object that you can put on the ground. Scatter these items in a random fashion.

4. Identify a start line and a finish line. The mines should be between the start and finish lines.

5. Ask one person to stand on the starting line, wearing a blindfold or closing their eyes. Their partner stands on the finish line.

6. The partners on the finish line verbally give directions to the blindfolded partners, instructing them to step around the mines while making their way to the finish line.

7. If a blindfolded partner steps on a mine, he or she has to go back to the starting line.

VARIATIONS

The group can go all at once, or one team can go at a time and they can be timed.

PROCESSING QUESTIONS

How did it feel to have to listen to and trust the verbal commands of your partner? Did they give good verbal communications? If not, what could they have done better? How did you do when you were the one communicating commands?

SCHOLASTIC SOCCER

GAME TYPE
Cooperation and communication; problem solving

MATERIALS
A small ball or something to pass

GROUP SIZE
10–20

TIME
10–20 minutes

OBJECTIVES
The object of this game is for students to work together as a team. You can use this game as a review for tests, quizzes, or current events.

INSTRUCTIONS
1. Find a wide-open space, such as a gym or an outdoor field.
2. Prepare a set of questions. These questions can be review questions for an upcoming test, questions from a recent chapter or unit, current event questions, or other similar questions.
3. Divide the class into two teams.
4. Position students around the room similar to the positioning of a soccer team, with defense, offense, midfield, and goalie.
5. Have them pair up with a member of the opposite team and stand face-to-face.

6. Start the ball in the hands of one team on the defensive side. (Other objects you have in class, such as an eraser or a tennis ball, could be used instead of a ball.)
7. If the defensive person with the ball answers the question correctly, he can pass it to another member on his team toward the opposing goal. They can only advance the ball one player forward.
8. The player with the ball now gets to answer a question.
9. When a person answers the question incorrectly, the ball goes to the opposing person from the other team facing him, and that player gets a question. If he answers it correctly, he then can advance the ball to a player in front of him.
10. A goal is scored when the person who is closest to the goal gets the answer correct and tosses the ball to the opposing goalie. The goalie gets a chance to defend the goal by correctly answering a question. If the goalie gets it wrong, a goal is scored.
11. The game continues with the ball going to the defensive end of the team that just gave up the point.

VARIATIONS

- You can challenge other classes to a scholastic bowl championship.
- You can make a rule that the ball cannot be passed to the same person twice until everyone from their team has had a chance to answer a question. This can make it frustrating, as they may have to pass it

backward to get the ball to the person who has not answered a question yet.

PROCESSING QUESTIONS

What frustrations did you feel during the game? Have you ever been on a team that did not work well together as a group? If so, how did you handle it?

TRUST FALL

GAME TYPE
Trust; cooperation and communication

MATERIALS
None

GROUP SIZE
10–15

TIME
20–40 minutes

OBJECTIVES
The objective of this game is to build trust among students. The trust fall is one of the hardest and most challenging of all team-building exercises. Some students may struggle with this activity.

INSTRUCTIONS
1. Divide the group into two. Create two lines of students facing each other. They should hold their arms out in a zipper pattern with the people across from them (see photo).
2. Talk to the group about the concept of spotting. Teach them that while playing this game, they will need to spot their classmates. Their legs must be bent, they have to be focused on the person falling, they cannot talk during the process, their hair needs to be pulled back, and they should not wear watches or jewelry.

3. Ask for a "brave" volunteer. Ask that student to stand on a desk or small platform, no higher than 3–4 feet.

4. Before each person does the trust fall, have them tell the group one thing that they are proud of and one thing that they are afraid of. These can be as simple as "I am proud of my family" and "I am afraid of not getting into college."

5. When the person is ready to do the trust fall, have them turn their back to the spotters.

6. Ask the volunteer to put their hands in their pockets or lock their fingers together with their arms straight so that when they fall they don't flail their arms and hit the spotters.

7. Once the volunteer is ready, they say out loud, "Spotters ready?"

8. If the spotters are ready, together they shout out, "Ready."

9. Instruct the person doing the trust fall to fall stiffly, like a tree.

10. Once the person doing the trust fall is in the arms of the spotters, slowly lower the person down feet first.

VARIATIONS

There are many variables in the trust-fall activity. If someone is struggling with this activity, it may take some time to encourage them to complete this. The game can be modified as a trust sit, where the person falls back into the team members' arms from the ground, rather than an elevated platform.

PROCESSING QUESTIONS

How did it feel to be up there and having to trust your group? How do you deal with trust in your life? What were your concerns? What did you learn about yourself in this activity? Why is trust so hard for people? Have you ever trusted someone and then they let you down? If so, how did you deal with it? What did you learn about your group today? Have you ever felt like you could not do something, but then achieved it? What was it? How did it feel?

TRUST JUMP

GAME TYPE
Trust; cooperation and communication

MATERIALS
None

GROUP SIZE
10–15

TIME
20–40 minutes

OBJECTIVES
The objective of this game is to build trust among students. The trust jump is one of the hardest and most challenging of all team-building exercises. Some students may struggle with this activity.

INSTRUCTIONS
1. Divide the group into two. Create two lines of students facing each other. They should hold their arms out in a zipper pattern with the people across from them (see photo).
2. Talk to the group about the concept of spotting. Teach them that while playing this game, they will need to spot their classmates. Their legs must be bent, they have to be focused on the person falling, they cannot talk during the process, their hair needs to be pulled back, and they should not wear watches or jewelry.

3. Ask for a "brave" volunteer. Ask that student to stand on a desk or small platform, no higher than 3–4 feet.
4. Before each person does the trust jump, have them tell the group one thing that they are proud of and one thing that they are afraid of. These can be as simple as "I am proud of my family" and "I am afraid of not getting into college."
5. When the person is ready to do the trust jump, have them turn their back to the spotters.
6. Ask the volunteer to put their hands in their pockets or lock their fingers together with their arms straight, so that when they fall they don't flail their arms and hit the spotters.
7. Once the volunteer is ready, they say out loud, "Spotters ready?"
8. If the spotters are ready, together they shout out, "Superman!"
9. Instruct the person doing the trust jump to jump out as far as they can.
10. Once the person doing the trust jump is in the arms of the spotters, slowly lower them down feet first.

VARIATIONS

Measure how far each student jumps.

PROCESSING QUESTIONS

How did it feel to be up there and having to trust your group? How do you deal with trust in your life? What were your concerns? What did you learn about yourself in this activity? Why is trust so hard for people? Have you ever trusted someone and then they let you down? If so, how did you deal with it? What did you learn about your group today? Have you ever felt like you could not do something, but then achieved it? What was it? How did it feel?

BLOB MACHINE

GAME TYPE
Cooperation and communication; trust, problem solving

MATERIALS
None

GROUP SIZE
10–15

TIME
15–45 minutes

OBJECTIVES
The objective is to get the students to work together as a group, increase trust, and achieve a team goal.

INSTRUCTIONS
1. Clear the desks in the room so you have an open area.
2. Tell the group that they are a blob machine and must get from point A to point B.
3. As a team, they must be connected at all times and are limited in the number of limbs (arms or legs) they can have touching the ground at any given point. You will decide how many limbs they can use. The fewer limbs, the harder it will be. A general rule is if there are 10 students (20 limbs), cut that number in half and subtract a few more. For example, for 10 students, use 7–8 limbs.

4. The group (blob machine) must work together to find a way to always be connected to each other while moving forward toward the designated finish line. If at any point they break contact with each other, or if too many limbs are touching the floor, they must start over. As a safety rule, don't allow anyone to get on another student's shoulders.

I have seen a hundred different ways this can be done. There will be a lot of failure at first, and lots of kids talking at one point, but the evolution of watching them work this out is a wonderful thing.

VARIATIONS

Depending on the group and their ability level, you may want to add or subtract limbs during the course of the activity.

PROCESSING QUESTIONS

How did it feel when your group was struggling? How do you usually deal with your frustration when you are struggling at something? Did you feel the group worked together? If not, what could have been done differently? Have you had a hard time with working in a group in the past? If so, when? What did you do to work through the difficulty?

GAME OF LIFE

GAME TYPE
Icebreaker; cooperation and communication; trust

MATERIALS
Tarp

GROUP SIZE
10–30

TIME
10–30 minutes

OBJECTIVES
Students will work with a team and solve problems.

INSTRUCTIONS
1. Give the group a tarp, the larger the better. Establish a starting line and a finish line.
2. Ask the students to hold all the corners of the tarp and start walking toward the finish line.
3. Along the way, shout out a real-life catastrophe or danger—for example, earthquake, shark, locusts, etc.. Each time there is a life event, the students need to stop and get on the tarp for safety. Every time the tarp is picked up again, the team needs to fold it in half.
4. See how small the tarp can go without them falling or stepping off the tarp.

VARIATIONS

Create a competition between groups to see which group can get the farthest without having to start over.

PROCESSING QUESTIONS

How did it feel as the tarp got smaller? Was your group frustrated at any point in this activity? Do you feel your group worked well together? How did you communicate instructions to the group? Did you feel supported by the group?

TARP BALL-TOSS

GAME TYPE
Icebreaker; cooperation and communication; trust

MATERIALS
Tarp, ball

GROUP SIZE
10–30

TIME
10–30 minutes

OBJECTIVES
Students will work with a team and solve problems.

INSTRUCTIONS
1. Place a ball (tennis ball, basketball, etc.) in the middle of a tarp.
2. Choose a starting line and a finish line.
3. Ask the students to get around the tarp and pick it up without the ball falling off.
4. The group can only advance forward when the ball is in the air. If it falls off the tarp, the group needs to go back to the starting line. You can do this with groups as a competition or as a class to see how fast you can make it to the finish line.

VARIATIONS
- You can have obstacles in the field (other students) that have to be navigated around.

- The students can close their eyes, with one person directing them while the ball is in the air.

PROCESSING QUESTIONS

Did your group work as a team? What were some of the frustrations the group had during this activity? Can you give an example in your life of when you had to work closely together with others to achieve a common goal?

TARP PING-PONG

GAME TYPE
Icebreaker; cooperation and communication; trust

MATERIALS
Tarp for each team, ball

GROUP SIZE
10–30

TIME
10–30 minutes

OBJECTIVES
Students will work with a team and solve problems.

INSTRUCTIONS
1. Divide the class into 2 teams.
2. Give each group a tarp.
3. Teams need to toss a ball from their tarp to the other tarp while moving from the starting line to the finish line.

VARIATIONS
Ask the students to move farther apart after every catch, or you can ask them to always move sideways as they throw and catch.

PROCESSING QUESTIONS
Did your group work as a team? What were some of the frustrations the group had during this activity? Can you give an example in your life of when you had to work closely together with others to achieve a common goal?

TARP HOLE IN ONE

GAME TYPE
Icebreaker; cooperation and communication; trust

MATERIALS
Tarp, ball

GROUP SIZE
10–30

TIME
10–30 minutes

OBJECTIVES
Students will work with a team and solve problems.

INSTRUCTIONS
1. Create targets on the floor or grass. These can be formed by using Hula-Hoops spaced randomly, or by strings in the shape of circles. You can assign points to targets, making smaller targets more valuable.
2. Using the tarp and ball, ask the students to launch a ball from the tarp to the designated target.

VARIATIONS
See how many points students can get in a given time period.

PROCESSING QUESTIONS

Did your group work as a team? What were some of the frustrations the group had during this activity? Can you give an example in your life of when you had to work closely together with others to achieve a common goal?

CENTIPEDE BODY-PASS

GAME TYPE
Icebreaker; trust; cooperation and communication; processing questions

MATERIALS
None

GROUP SIZE
10–20

TIME
15–45 minutes

OBJECTIVES
The objective is to increase trust among classmates.

INSTRUCTIONS
1. Ask the students to lie on the floor or grass, on their backs, head to head, alternating sides.
2. Ask everyone on the floor to put his or her arms in the air like a centipede lying on its back.
3. Pick one person who will lie down, face up, with their arms crossed across chest.
4. The group will slowly pass the person down the line until they make it to the end of the line.

VARIATIONS
- Multiple groups can compete at one time go and make it a race.

- Have the person being passed close their eyes.

PROCESSING QUESTIONS

What did it feel like to be passed by the group? Did you trust them not to drop you? What were some of your concerns in doing this activity? Is trust a hard thing for you? If so, why?

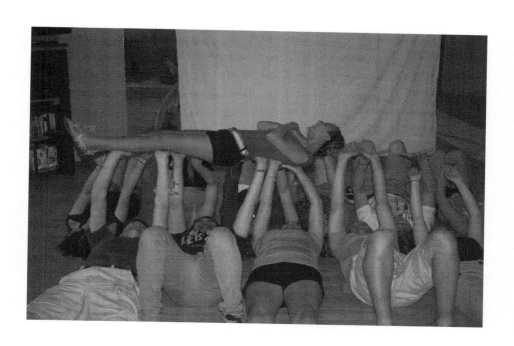

225

LIKE AN EGYPTIAN

GAME TYPE
Trust; icebreaker; cooperation and communication; problem solving

MATERIALS
None

GROUP SIZE
2–3 groups of 8–12

TIME
10–20 minutes

OBJECTIVE
Students will work as a team.

INSTRUCTIONS
1.   Form 2 or 3 groups.
2.   Talk about the Egyptians and describe how, in order to build the pyramids, they had to move massive blocks of stone over long distances. They moved those blocks by laying timber down side by side, and placing the blocks on top of the timber. By pulling the massive stones over the logs and replacing the last log, the block passed over to the front of the line so the block could continue its path.
3.   Explain to students that they will be the logs and block. They must lie down side by side, close together, and place a block (one the members of their team) and roll together as

a unit. They must move the block (the team member with them) toward a finish line.

4. The first team to get its block over the determined finish line wins.

5. You can do this activity in the hallway, outside, or in the gym.

6. The person who represents the block is usually the smallest member in the group, for obvious reasons

7. The team member who is the block should lie on their back with their arms crossed across their chest.

8. If the block (person) touches the ground, the entire group has to start over.

PROCESSING QUESTIONS

Talk with the group about the frustrations they may have had in trying to work together as a team: What were some of the things that surprised you about this activity? Who was the leader? How was the leader chosen? Did the group listen to the leader? If not, why?

TRUST RUN

GAME TYPE
Trust; cooperation and communication

MATERIALS
None

GROUP SIZE
10–15

TIME
15–30 minutes

OBJECTIVES
The objective is for students to trust that their group will raise their hands as they approach running toward them. This helps students learn to work together as a group to support the person running.

INSTRUCTIONS
1. Divide the class into 2 groups.
2. You will need an open area such as a hallway, gym, or field for this activity.
3. Arrange groups into two straight lines facing each other.
4. Ask the students to extend their arms out straight, intertwining them like a zipper with the person across from them.
5. Ask one student to be the "runner." They will face the group and give the commands.
6. The runner will yell, "Spotters ready?"

7. If all the spotters reply with a "yes," the runner begins running toward the group whose arms are extended out.

8. As the runner approaches the group, the people closest to the runner raise their hands in the air as fast as they can. The next people in line do the same as the runner approaches their outstretched hands. If they do not raise their arms fast enough, the runner will run into their hands. (This is like a wave.). As the runner approaches, the arms go up.

9. Repeat with each member of the group.

VARIATIONS

None

PROCESSING QUESTIONS

When you were running toward the group, did you trust that they would raise their arms in enough time so you would not get hit? If not, why? What was your greatest fear in doing this activity? What other things have you been afraid of doing? Why? When you have fear, how do you handle it?

CIRCLE UP

GAME TYPE
Icebreaker; cooperation and communication

MATERIALS
None

GROUP SIZE
10–50

TIME
10–20 minutes

OBJECTIVES
The objective of this game is to encourage teamwork.

INSTRUCTIONS
1. Have the group form a circle.
2. Ask the students to place their right foot next to the foot of the person on their right, and their left foot next to the foot of the person on their left.
3. Without breaking the contacts with their feet, have them begin to walk around to the right as a group. If any feet break contact, the group needs to start over.
4. Once the group has completed a full circle, have them reverse the direction of the circle.

VARIATIONS
*   Have the group do the activity with their eyes closed.

- Have a caller periodically call out reverses.

PROCESSING QUESTIONS
Did your group work well together? If not, why?

TOWER WARS

GAME TYPE
Icebreaker; cooperation and communication

MATERIALS
Playing cards or index cards

GROUP SIZE
10–30

TIME
20 minutes

OBJECTIVES
The objective is for students to work together and communicate within a group.

INSTRUCTIONS
1. Divide your class or group into teams of 4–8.
2. Give each group a deck of playing cards or index cards.
3. Tell each group that they have 20 minutes to build a tower with their cards.
4. Awards will be given to the highest tower and the most creative tower (as judged by you).

VARIATIONS
- You can have teams of two combining groups to challenge other groups.
- Ask all the groups to combine their cards to create one giant castle.

PROCESSING QUESTIONS

When your cards fell down, how did your group react? Who was the leader of your group? Who chose the leader? Were they a good leader? Were your ideas heard?

REASSEMBLE THE STORY

GAME TYPE
Icebreaker; cooperation and communication; problem solving

MATERIALS
Old books or magazines

GROUP SIZE
Groups of 4–6

TIME
15–40 minutes

OBJECTIVES
The objective is for students to communicate and work together in a group in putting the books or newspaper back together in the right order.

INSTRUCTIONS
1. Find old books that you no longer use. These books can be old children's books, old short novels (the shorter the better), or old newspapers.
2. Cut off or blacken out the numbers on the pages.
3. If you can find 3–4 of the same books or newspapers, that would work best (one for each team).
4. Mix up the pages and give them to each group.
5. See how fast they can reassemble the story, book, or newspaper in the right order.

VARIATIONS

- You can use just one book for the whole class, with each group getting a random chapter. See which group puts their chapter together first.

- If you use a small children's book (less then 25 pages) you can have the groups read their chapter to the class when all the groups have put their chapters together.

PROCESSING QUESTIONS

What frustrations did you have doing this activity? Why? Do you feel your group worked well together? If not, why? Was there one role of leader in the group? If so, who chose the leader? What was your role in the group? Were you happy with it?

WE ARE WHAT WE ARE

GAME TYPE
Icebreaker; problem solving; trust

MATERIALS
Name tags and a pen

GROUP SIZE
10–25

TIME
10–30 minutes

OBJECTIVE
The objective is for students to understand what it is like to be treated by others based on how people see them.

INSTRUCTIONS
1. On each name tag, write an adjective that describes people or emotions, such as happy, sad, pushover, selfish, shy, insecure, boastful, or angry. Other statements can be included, such as, "Laugh at me," "Ignore me," "Treat me like I don't exist," "Treat me like I am famous," "Treat me like I just did something very bad," etc. Any adjective or description can be used. You can also ask the class to come up with a list you can write on the board, and also have them written on name tags.
2. Once all the emotions and behaviors have been put on name tags, ask the students to

come up one at a time and pick a tag at random.

3. Once the name tags have been picked, ask the students to attach the card to their shirt and walk around the class.

4. Every time they come up to someone with a name tag, they must treat the other person like their name tag designates. For example, if they are wearing a name tag that says "Ignore me," you will walk up to them, look at them as if they did not exist, and walk away. If they are wearing a name tag that says "happy," you should treat them as you would a happy person.

VARIATIONS

- Do this activity for 15 minutes. Then, instead of treating people like the word, adjective, or action on their card, you must now talk or act like the word or adjective on your own name tag and greet the people with it.
- You can use famous people, sports figures, history or literature figures you have been studying.

PROCESSING QUESTIONS

Were you happy with the name tag you drew? If not, why? How did it feel to have people treat you based solely on your name tag? What were your emotions when other people treated you based on your name tag? Have you ever treated someone solely based on how they looked to you or acted to you, or on your perception of them? If so, when? Would you treat them differently now?

BAD DAY

GAME TYPE
Problem solving; cooperation and communication; trust

MATERIALS
Paper and pen

GROUP SIZE
10–20

TIME
10–20 minutes

OBJECTIVES
The objective is for students to share with their peers some of the struggles that they go through, and to see that there may be alternative ways to dealing with their personal struggles. Students can see that other people have similar problems and that they, too, find ways to get through them.

INSTRUCTIONS
1. Talk with your class about how each of us has had "bad" days in our lives.
2. Ask your students to write on a piece of paper their worst day, or a bad day they have recently.
3. Once they are finished, ask them to pass it to the person behind them.
4. As each person gets someone else's bad-day paper, they will write down a brief description of what they would have done if

that had been their bad day or situation. Have them give suggestions on what they could have done, or just offer a kind comment.
5.   Keep this going until the paper gets back to the original owner. Due to time, you may want to limit how long you do this, or just do it by rows.

VARIATIONS

*   Have your students write down their toughest day and turn them in without their names on them. Read a couple of problems a week and talk about how the class would deal with those issues.
*   Pick out one "bad day" a week and have students volunteer to act out the scene, with a positive solution to the bad-day moment.

PROCESSING QUESTIONS

Did any of the suggestions you got make sense to you? Have you thought of those solutions before? Were any of the bad-day moments that were passed to you similar to yours? How did it feel to try to help someone else out with his or her bad-day moments? Do you think that you may be better at dealing with your bad-day moments now that you have other ways to deal with your bad-day moments? Are you willing to listen to others when it comes to your problems?

NITRO

GAME TYPE
Trust; cooperation and communication; problem solving

MATERIALS
Paper cup and water

GROUP SIZE
Groups of 4–6

TIME
15–40 minutes

OBJECTIVES
The object is for students to work together as a group to turn their teammate around without spilling a drop of "nitro." This encourages students to trust each other and work together as a group.

INSTRUCTIONS
1. Put the class in groups of 4–6.
2. Give each team a paper cup filled ¾ full of water. Tell the class that the water represents nitroglycerin. If one drop is spilled, they all will blow up.
3. One person is in the middle with the cup of "nitro." The rest of the group circles around them.
4. The object is to turn the person all the way around—upside down and back to standing without spilling a drop of "nitro." Spotting and safety are essential here.

VARIATIONS

- Compete as groups to see who can achieve the goal first.
- Blindfold the person holding the "nitro."
- Have every member of the group complete the task. The first group to get everyone to complete the task first wins.

PROCESSING QUESTIONS

Were you ever afraid during this activity? Did you ever not feel safe during this activity? If so, why? When you are scared, how do you react or deal with it? What was the hardest thing about this activity? Did you feel your group worked well together?

26682057R00138

Made in the USA
Lexington, KY
11 October 2013